What No One Ever Tells You About

FINANCING YOUR OWN BUSINESS

Real-Life Financing Advice from
101 Successful Entrepreneurs

Jan Norman

Dearborn™
Trade Publishing
A **Kaplan Professional** Company

This publication is designed to provide accurate and authoritative information in regard to the subject matter covered. It is sold with the understanding that the publisher is not engaged in rendering legal, accounting, or other professional service. If legal advice or other expert assistance is required, the services of a competent professional person should be sought.

President, Dearborn Publishing: Roy Lipner
Vice President and Publisher: Cynthia A. Zigmund
Acquisitions Editor: Jonathan Malysiak
Development Editor: Karen Murphy
Interior Design: Lucy Jenkins
Cover Design: Scott Rattray, Rattray Design
Typesetting: Elizabeth Pitts

Printed in the United States of America

05 06 07 10 9 8 7 6 5 4 3 2 1

Library of Congress Cataloging-in-Publication Data

Norman, Jan.
    What no one ever tells you about financing your own business : real-life financing advice from 101 successful entrepreneurs / Jan Norman.
        p. cm.
    Includes bibliographical references and index.
    ISBN 1-4195-0277-8 (alk. paper)
    1. Corporations—Finance. 2. Business enterprises—Finance. 3. New business enter-prises—Finance.   I. Title: Financing your own business.   II. Title.
    HG4026.N67   2005
    658.15′22—dc2
                                                                            2005001075

CONTENTS

SECTION F: THE PUBLIC MARKETS

The title of this book has a double meaning. This book details 101 sources of business capital, the preparation to seek it, and the common ways of making the most of the money that an entrepreneur has. These sources are not theoretical. These are real businesses that actually have employed these sources and methods. But this book also resembles an introductory course—colleges often number such courses 101—in the range of capital sources that businesses manage to tap into when getting started, surviving, and growing. If you want step-by-step details of how to apply for a bank loan or win venture capital, other books will be more help. This book should stimulate your creative thinking about means and methods for financing your own business.

I wrote this book after years of fielding questions from experienced business owners as well as budding entrepreneurs about potential sources of money for businesses. I have sought answers from hundreds of business owners all over the country. This book provides the most plausible, useful answers from real businesses that succeeded in acquiring capital from these sources. No one source is sufficient for every need throughout every company's life span. Every one of the companies in this book has used multiple methods for acquiring capital. Not every source described in this book is available to every business. Some programs or sources are limited to certain types of businesses or to specific geographic regions. You might reject some sources as undesirable for your individual business. For example, you might not want to give up control in order to receive equity capital.

While reading this book, do not ignore the integrity, sacrifice, and persistence required to finance a business. Starting and running a business is hard work. Don't expect anyone to give you business capital for nothing. Do expect to put your own money on the line repeatedly in order to keep the business going and to attract other sources of capital. Do expect to think creatively when capital runs low or outside sources dry up.

Money alone isn't the object of financing your own business. The first section of this book explores the groundwork you must lay to make your business ready for and worthy of receiving capital. Such steps as writing a business plan, which are wise for any entrepreneur, are essential when seeking outside capital for a company. The second section describes capital sources most available to businesses in the formative stages. You must be most creative in financing during the early years because relatively few people and institutions with money are willing to take a chance on an unproven venture. The third section stresses the importance of wise use of money and the need to continually monitor the financial health of your business to avert a cash crisis and to avoid wasting precious capital. The fourth section shows that established businesses usually have a greater variety of choices than start-ups, but also must continue to use some of the sources most often tapped by beginners, such as personal savings, family, and friends. Throughout the book, business owners stress the importance of relationships in financing their companies. While many relatives, friends, bankers, lenders, and equity partners will go to great lengths to help a company, they expect honest communication and full disclosure about the beneficiary of their funds. Successful entrepreneurs realize that these capital sources are allies, not enemies, and treat them with respect and candor.

ACKNOWLEDGMENTS

I am so grateful to the many business owners and financial experts who have shared their strategies and methods with me, for this book specifically and more generally to help me better understand their businesses, loans, and investments.

I greatly appreciate the assistance of those who helped me find business owners to share their stories about business capital and insights into obtaining and maximizing capital. I am indebted to my brother, Jim Norman, executive director of the Phoenix Creative Planning Centers Foundation in Phoenix, Arizona; Linda Pinson, owner of Out of Your Mind and Into the Marketplace in Tustin, California; and Suzanne Martin of Suzanne Martin Inc. in Waxahachie, Texas. I also thank the U.S. Small Business Administration, National Association for the Self-Employed, Young Entrepreneurs Organization, Venture Alliance, ACCION USA, Washington CASH, U-Start business incubator, Tech Coast Angels, Ford Motor Co. Building Entrepreneurial Success Today, Southland Economic Development Corporation, ShoreBank Pacific, State of Montana, State of Arizona, Microsoft, and SJF Ventures.

PART 1

TOOLS FOR
ATTRACTING CAPITAL

■ ■ ■

It is the rare company that attracts start-up or growth capital without asking for it. The vast majority of businesses must lay the groundwork to be perceived worthy of a loan or equity investment. Money doesn't just fall out of the sky into the open arms of a waiting entrepreneur. The owner must first acquire or create the tools that will attract needed capital.

The universal tool, whether you seek a loan or equity, is the business plan. Virtually every financial institution or investor wants to know how much money your company needs, how you will repay the money, and how your company will grow enough to be able to repay the money. Their first concern isn't your business's success. It is getting their money back, plus a profit for them. The business plan should answer those questions. Lenders and investors usually measure your company by its leadership. Many professionals consider the management team to be the most reliable means for determining whether a company can achieve the goals for which it seeks capital. They invest in people, not ideas or companies per se.

Sometimes entrepreneurs don't get the loan or equity they seek and have no idea why. It is helpful to have disinterested professionals evaluate the business and its plan for weaknesses and stumbling blocks. However, the business owner or management team should write their own business plan and not delegate the task to consultants or a staff member. The owner must understand the business in order to convince the sources of capital that he or she is capable of delivering the promises in a business plan.

In addition to a written business plan, a company should have at least the beginning of infrastructure to demonstrate that the plan is more than a good idea. A company that has an office, accountant, attorney, and board of advisors; is delivering products or services; and has paying customers will qualify for more capital than one that is still in the formative stage. Such a company will pay lower interest rates on loans or will have to give away less equity than a company that exists merely on paper.

Relationships are also vital tools in obtaining capital. People do business with people they know and trust. The entrepreneur who has developed relationships with equity investors or lenders is more likely to get needed capital than a stranger. If the entrepreneur lacks the right connections, he or she must bring on board accountants, attorneys, and other professional advisors who can make the right introductions to the loan and investment decision makers.

1. THE BUSINESS PLAN'S ROLE IN THE CAPITAL SEARCH

A business without a written plan is unlikely to
attract outside investment or loans.

■ ■ ■

When Tom Wacker was considering whether to buy Best Made
Mattress Inc. in Denver, Colorado, he wrote a business plan for the mattress manufacturer. It was a habit he developed as a venture capitalist with
Centaur Holdings Corp. The business plans Wacker has written with business planning software called "Automate Your Business Plan" by Out of
Your Mind and Into the Marketplace in Tustin, California, have raised $22
million for several different companies.

For Best Made Mattress, Tom wrote three different versions of the plan
before he even bought the company. The negotiations stretched over 18
months, which spanned a recession and the terrorist attacks of September
11, 2001, and forced dramatic rethinking of the deal.

"I don't write a plan just to get capital," Tom says. "I need a plan so I
know which road I'm on."

A business plan serves several purposes. It helps entrepreneurs to understand what business they are really in and how best to run the company.
It builds the case for any loan or equity the company seeks. And it plots an
exit strategy for the owner. Every company needs a written business plan
but relatively few have one, and some that do don't follow the plan. Linda
Pinson, creator of "Automate Your Business Plan," says the plan must be
consistent throughout. The financial documents must reflect decisions
spelled out in the organizational and marketing sections of the plan.

Tom insists the business owner should write the plan, not delegate the
task to an employee or outside consultant. "If I'm going for funding, it
doesn't matter if it's a local banker or a venture capitalist, they don't know
my business. I have to educate them and to do that I need to know it myself."

Because the business world is so dynamic, the business plan must be
continually revised, Tom says. He has written another ten versions of the
plan for Best Made Mattress since he closed the transaction in November
2002. That work made Tom aware that his industry was changing. When he

first bought the company, Best Made Mattress sold to distributors. Then Best Made Mattress started selling directly to retailers. More recently, Tom's business plan research convinced him that Best Made Mattress needed to further evolve to sell directly to consumers, a change made in 2004.

"My job, as a business owner, is to be profitable," Tom says. "Business changes fast so I can't say, 'this is how business will be in three years.' I have to have the vision to know what's happening in my industry and adjust. The business plan enables me to do that."

With a revised business plan in hand, Tom went to a banker for the $500,000 needed to move to a location suitable for both manufacturing and retailing. "Writing the plan helps me work out the mistakes rather than make them," he says. "When I give a bank a business plan, it can get all the way through underwriting."

The business plan must be written for a target audience. Tom doesn't want equity investors at this point, so he stresses the historical financials that bankers look at when making a loan decision. Once he grows annual sales to $44 million, either Tom or a potential buyer will revise the plan to define ways Best Made Mattress can grow to sales of $500 million through international expansion. That step will require an equity investor, such as a multinational corporation or public stock offering.

"When I was young I didn't know people would give you money for business and then come in and fire you," Tom says. "When I'm ready to be fired, I'll write the plan for equity investment."

2. SCORING YOUR PLAN

Get feedback on the strength of the specifics of your
business plan important to investors or lenders
before making your official presentations.

■ ■ ■

DayNa Decker and Muguet Houston founded Lumetique in Los Angeles, California, in 2001 to create products that combine oil lamps, fragrance, and attractive statuary. The lights are not only attractive but use patented wicks and clean-burning, water-soluble, nontoxic fuel. "It's the first innovation in candles for thousands of years," Muguet says.

Combining their money with family contributions, the pair developed a product line and applied for patents, but they knew they would need more money to get the candles into high-fashion stores and for marketing. They developed a business plan and started making the rounds of individual private investors.

Very-early-stage entrepreneurs struggle to get meetings with potential investors and often come away empty handed in more ways than one—no funding and no idea how the potential investor rated the company. Such entrepreneurs rarely get a second chance to make a favorable impression. They go from presentation to presentation with little or no feedback to help them make adjustments and improvements. Because of the time it takes to read and evaluate a business plan, most venture capitalists read portions of only 20 percent of the plans they receive. They fund only one out of a hundred plans they do read.

One of DayNa and Muguet's stops was with executives of Venture Alliance, a nationwide network of venture capitalists, investment bankers, business advisors, and technical experts who look for the best equity investments regardless of size or location. Founders James Casparie and John Garcia have evaluated thousands of entrepreneurial ventures over the years and from that experience have developed a patented evaluation process designed to dig out success indicators that aren't necessarily evident in a business plan. Through an extensive list of questions, a company is rated on 12 factors: market opportunity, marketing and sales strategy, competition, entrepreneurial experience, management team, founder commitment, board of directors or advisors, financials and pricing, valuation and use of funds, accomplishments, corporate structure, and intellectual property. Some entrepreneurs can't answer the questions and others won't take the time. DayNa and Muguet did.

Venture Alliance likens the evaluation to credit scoring of individual consumers that enables lenders to evaluate the creditworthiness of thousands of borrowers quickly. Lenders know that a consumer with a FICO (Fair Isaac Corp.) score of 800 will get a loan and one with a score of less than 500 either won't get a loan or must pay a higher interest rate. Venture Alliance's scoring enables its network of investors just as quickly to evaluate the investment-worthiness of many more companies than they could by just reading the business plans. The Venture Alliance–scored information is the same as provided in business plans but in different form.

The evaluation and score also helps entrepreneurs spot their strengths and weaknesses. It gives specific areas on which to work in order to become more attractive to investors. Lumetique's greatest strengths are its intellectual property and market opportunity. Its weakness is its management team because such an early-stage company is still trying to attract strong executives with specific experience needed to help raise capital. "It's a matter of which comes first when you need both a strong management team and capital," Muguet says.

The average company that receives equity investment earns a 70 percent score on Venture Alliance's 1,200-point scale. In April 2003, Lumetique earned 741 points, or 62 percent. Its intellectual property and market opportunity were good, but DayNa's experience and the management team were weak.

DayNa and Muguet started working on building up Lumetique in those areas that scored low. Seventeen months later the company scored 841 on Venture Alliance's scale and subsequently received funding from Angel Strategies, a California-based seed capital investor for high-wealth individuals, and Palladium, a New York investment banker.

"The scoring was quite helpful," says Muguet who has previously raised money for other technology companies. "Often when we present to individuals, they don't ask the right questions so they don't get the information they need to make an investment decision."

3. BUILD INFRASTRUCTURE

Strengthening your management team, vendor network,
and customer base will turn an unfunded venture into
a profitable and investment-attractive company.

■ ■ ■

While managing the use of private airplanes in the late 1990s, Nate McKelvey noticed great inefficiencies in leasing private, luxury jet aircraft. Customers had to pay for a round-trip even when they only needed to fly one way. At the same time, 30 percent to 40 percent of chartered planes flew empty on some legs of their trips. Nate proposed to match customers and airplanes in his company, CharterAuction.com in Quincy, Massachusetts. The company offers fixed, per-hour fees, and then opens an individual's flight request to its network of jet operators. They can bid for the job in an online reverse auction with the fixed fee as the ceiling price. The savings are passed on to the customer.

Competing concepts had raised tens of millions of dollars from venture capitalists.

"When I started looking for capital in November 1999, I thought it was a great time, but behind the scenes venture capitalists had already started cutting back," Nate says. "I couldn't get outside funding, so I gave up on the idea of raising capital and focused on making a living at this business."

Nate dug in and started CharterAuction.com in borrowed office space with $60,000 in savings, his own software consulting fees, and his wife's salary. Nate did his own software programming. Most significantly, he used his experiences as a pilot and as a salesman to build a network of aircraft operators willing to provide flights for CharterAuction.com customers.

"There are 3,000 of these small, management companies in the United States, mostly owned by pilots," Nate says. "I'm a pilot as well, so I speak their language."

He telephoned flight managers explaining his concept and proposal. Most were initially skeptical, but Nate persisted until he signed up a thousand vendors.

"Even in a hot market there are always empty flights available and [CharterAuction.com's] money goes right to their bottom line," Nate says. "It was a matter of building personal relationships."

Eventually, CharterAuction.com trimmed its vendor list to 250 companies with the best safety records, customer service, and luxury facilities. Nate's hard work building strong relationships with quality vendors paid off. Company revenues grew more than 8,800 percent from 2000 to 2004, and the business was profitable. Customer Roger Vasey, a retired Merrill Lynch executive, was so impressed with CharterAuction.com's concept and service that he and other customers invested $2 million in the company.

"I flew with CharterAuction several times and liked the experience so much, I asked to meet the owner," Roger says. "I have made a number of investments over the years in small companies, some successful, some not. None is as exciting as this one."

The investors demanded that CharterAuction.com continue to build a professional infrastructure, Nate says, so he has improved the computer system that runs the auctions, introduced policies and procedures, and created a concierge department to enhance customer service even more. Staff more than doubled to 30 in 2003.

"I saw I wasn't going to be a dominant player without making the company more professional," Nate says.

As a result, venture capitalists have started calling.

"I asked, 'Where were you when I needed you?'" Nate laughs.

4. EVALUATE AVAILABLE RESOURCES

Before seeking capital, consider which potential source
could gain the most from your enterprise.

■ ■ ■

Peter Cunningham has started two public relations companies and a real estate investment firm with more than a dozen separate limited liability companies (LLCs) representing different apartment deals. Each time, he sifted through the potential sources of capital. And with each success, those choices increased. The entrepreneur's tendency is to focus on what the company needs, "but always think in terms of what's a win-win for the investor as well as for you," Pete says. The more you can offer, the wider your variety of capital sources. Weigh each for its suitability for the project at hand.

Like most first-time business start-ups, Pete had to use his own money for his first public relations firm, Beacon Communications in Chicago, Illinois. He sold that company and in 2002 met a group of businesspeople willing to put up 30 percent of the capital for a firm specifically servicing business-to-business financial clients.

"What I found was that I had been my own boss too long, so I bought them out," Pete says of Cunningham & Company LLC.

In 2002, Pete and two partners also started CCR Investments to buy apartments. Early success with little projects attracted increasingly large investors, opened doors to government financing, and even improved the capital opportunities for his public relations firm. Within two years CCR bought 400 apartment units in 13 different limited liability companies.

A lender makes a home mortgage based on the buyer's income. For a small apartment deal, the lender also considers anticipated rental income. If other investors participate, their balance sheets bolster the loan application so the LLC needs less money for a down payment and can buy bigger buildings. Initially CCR gave investors 12 percent interest on their capital and 60 percent of profits from rental income. After investors made back their initial investment plus interest, their passive income dropped to 40 percent and CCR received 60 percent. With the success of initial LLCs, CCR was able to drop investors' interest rate to 8 percent because it was apparent that CCR could deliver successful ventures.

Pete went through his Rolodex of businesspeople and attorneys with capital to invest. An attorney friend introduced Pete to a couple of other wealthy men who wanted to invest in income property but didn't know how. "After the first couple of deals, our buildings were performing really well so the banks started looking at us differently," Pete says. Banks provided a guidance line, like a line of credit, so CCR could pay cash, which commanded the lowest sales price. CCR improved the building and filled all apartments with renters before obtaining a mortgage. The improvements increased the building's value 30 percent to 40 percent; so in essence, CCR was buying the building with no money down. Within two years, CCR's assets under management were growing 2,500 percent a year.

The early successes attracted institutional investors with even greater capital clout. When CCR started buying larger buildings, it needed an investment bank instead of a commercial bank. Bigger projects also open the door to government financing. "Chicago has $500 million to subsidize buying and rehabilitating housing property," Pete says. "This preferred financing is available in low-income areas where we have been investing. But it also requires expert attorneys who have figured out tax increment financing and tax-exempt bonds."

CCR's real estate success helps Cunningham & Company as well, Pete says. "I'm able to get fantastic financing for my PR firm because of the credibility built up by my real estate success. I'm the kind of guy who likes to pay cash for things, but [company] growth may require acquisitions, which I'm now able to finance."

5. BUILD PROFESSIONAL RELATIONSHIPS

Young companies can bolster their search for capital by
enlisting the help of professional advisors who
have credibility with money sources.

Nicolas Thomley's grandfather worked for a state rehabilitation services agency and every holiday meal included guests with various disabilities. After a stint in the Marines, Nick decided to open Pinnacle Services Inc. in Saint Louis Park, Minnesota, as a for-profit company to provide residential and vocational services for people with disabilities.

"After the initial $25,000 investment from personal savings and family, we quickly realized we needed a significant amount more because our business was growing rapidly," Nick says. "The problem was that my company had no financial history other than a few months of financial statements, and the company had no assets. I personally had no assets because I was a 21-year-old college student."

Nick turned to his accountant and attorney who had helped him set up Pinnacle Services and file incorporation papers. These older professionals had strong reputations and professional relationships in the community, which proved invaluable in Pinnacle Services's search for a bank line of credit. Nick had an especially strong relationship with his accountant, who had handled family tax matters in the past.

These connections don't have to be cultivated in a calculated manner. "I didn't sit down and write up a plan to build these relationships," Nick says. "They were just the right guys to work with who I knew for some time. Based on my accountant and attorney's relationship with a bank and my grandmother's willingness to put up one of her homes as collateral, I was able to secure a line of credit.

"Even with the collateral, the bank would not have done the line of credit without the relationships of my accountant and attorney," he adds.

Most entrepreneurs start with too few personal resources to build their companies by themselves. The greater their need for capital, the greater their need for established professionals who will make introductions to financial sources and vouch for the entrepreneurs and fledgling enterprises.

For some, family ties introduce them to these professional advisors. For others, contacts can be made through college, business organizations, friends, or their job. However, introductions aren't enough. Professionals won't risk their reputations on people they don't know. It's easier to establish credibility if the relationship starts with a personal introduction from a relative or friend. But quickly, the entrepreneur must cultivate the relationship with consideration, open communication, and proof through actions of being worthy of the professional's recommendation to capital sources.

Nick, with his college degree in organizational management and communication, spent two years laying the foundation for Pinnacle Services before starting services in January 2001. The company picked up referrals slowly at first. After a change in state law, Pinnacle Services grew from 6 to 130 clients in three months.

"I built a solid relationship with my professional advisors during this time, especially my accountant," Nick says. "We played golf together. This was before the need for the line of credit. Those relationships have gotten stronger over time. I take vacations with my accountant to Florida."

As for the lien on his grandmother's house, "We have gotten beyond that," he says. "The lien was not released for more than a year but it was enough to get things going."

Today, Pinnacle Services serves 175 people through group homes, community involvement, activities with peers, and respite care to give their families a break.

6. CULTIVATE YOUR NETWORK

Understanding the financial needs and goals of professional
acquaintances will strengthen your ability to tap this
network for capital when the time is right.

■ ■ ■

Investment banker Lew Alton decided to start another company after the dot-com crash in 2000 brought work to a halt for firms like his that assisted companies with their stock offerings to the public. This new company, CIC Group LLC in Scottsdale, Arizona, would buy companies with annual revenues in the $100 million range earned either from manufacturing products for or delivering services to the construction industry. CIC Group isn't interested in acquiring start-ups, companies on the verge of bankruptcy, or contractors. In addition to this specific niche, CIC Group is different in two ways. Competitors buy only one type of business in any geographic location. CIC Group considers a variety of businesses as long as they are located in the southwestern United States. Second, competitors raise money and then look for deals. CIC Group finds the deals and then seeks investments from large institutional investors such as pension plans.

Lew's background makes him unusually capable to run CIC Group in this way. As a Silicon Valley investment banker, he had published financial research reports on a thousand public companies. His firm had underwritten the public stock offerings for 500 companies. That expertise and experience had built for Lew a strong and wide network of fund managers and professional investors who trusted his word and knowledge. Many of these colleagues are now watching the deals that Lew is scouting.

"These investors trust me on what a deal will do; that's my expertise," Lew says. "I think my reputation is helpful with institutional investors."

Anyone seeking capital for a business opportunity can learn from Lew's approach. When money is involved, relationships are important. And relationships are built through professionalism and delivering on promises over time.

CIC Group's first deal illustrates the importance of a financial network to raise capital at any point of a company's life. Lew met the president of G-L Industries LLC in Magna, Utah, which manufactures wood laminated timbers, popularly called "glulam" beams, for commercial buildings. Glulam beams have the look of natural wood but greater strength, lower cost, and are available in longer lengths than real wood.

"I explained that I was looking for businesses to buy, and he said, 'What about mine?'" Lew says. "The only way this deal could do well was to have a strategic partner, not just institutional investors."

The most obvious strategic partner Lew could think of was Schuck and Sons Construction Co. Inc. in Glendale, Arizona, which supplies building components to commercial contractors. Schuck hadn't even considered such an alliance until Lew pointed out that the construction supplier could save 10 percent to 15 percent through G-L Industries. In most of CIC Group's deals, Lew expects to earn an ongoing management fee overseeing the investment for its professional funds and a significant portion of the profit after a company sells, typically within four to seven years. However the G-L Industries deal made so much sense for Schuck that it wanted to buy all of G-L Industries instead of being just a strategic partner.

Although CIC Group earned a lesser return on this project, Lew is pleased. "This was a bellwether deal to have something to show others for future transactions. And it's a matter of trust that there will be other deals in the future with Schuck. This business relies on trust."

PART 2

START-UP CAPITAL

■ ■ ■

I could retire if I received a dollar every time an aspiring entrepreneur asked for sources of grants to start a business. In fact, that's the most common question asked of the toll-free Answer Desk of the U.S. Small Business Administration. Grants imply free, gratis, no strings attached, no repayment needed. Honestly, who's going to give money for an untested idea to a person inexperienced in running a business?

Acquiring the capital for a new business is one of the most difficult tasks facing the entrepreneur. Banks want companies to have two to three years of profitable track record before approving a loan. So loans usually are personally guaranteed: credit cards, home equity loans, and even community development microloans. After talking with hundreds of business owners all over the country for years, it's obvious that some financial institutions are friendlier to fledgling entrepreneurs than others. The same is true of other likely sources of start-up capital. Some families would hock everything to help finance a relative's venture; some wouldn't invest a dime in a life-or-death situation. Some friends are eager to help; others flatly refuse.

In the absence of institutional capital and loans, the start-up entrepreneur must be creative and thrifty. Virtually all the business owners mentioned in this book had to put personal capital into their ventures, especially in the early stages. Consider some of the ways these owners acquired that capital: They sold personal possessions, cashed out retirement savings, tapped their talents, worked multiple jobs, entered contests, and more. Equally important, they were disciplined in diverting money from other desires to their business dreams and in managing undercapitalized companies.

Some communities and states have financing programs for businesses. A few examples are included in this book, but scout around your geographic area for ones that might help your company. Just be aware of the reasons politicians are willing to put public tax money into private businesses. They expect that they are investing in more jobs, economic growth, and poverty alleviation. Your business idea will need to provide those results in order to qualify for most public programs.

SECTION A

HELP YOURSELF BEFORE ASKING OTHERS

■ ■ ■

People who have a passion or necessity to start a business often find personal resources they didn't think about previously. It's not always about how much money you need to get started, but how little can you get by with. Fledgling business owners turn to their own piggy bank, work extra jobs, start their business part time, or tighten their belt so they can live on a spouse's salary while getting a new venture off the ground. They may even put their future retirement at risk by tapping pensions and retirement savings accounts.

These personal investments are usually crucial in seeking outside funding. Outsiders don't want to risk their money with someone who's not willing to put his own money on the line.

7. START ON A SHOESTRING

A business can be started with an
incredibly small amount of capital.

■ ■ ■

The next time someone tells you she doesn't have enough money to start a business, tell her about Mama Dip. That's the nickname for Mildred Edna Cotton Council, owner of Mama Dip's Kitchen in Chapel Hill, North Carolina.

Mama was a child during the Depression. From age four, she picked beans to sell in town. She learned about hard work, swapping beans for sugar, and selling what people needed—ice in summer and coal in winter—from her father who raised eight children after his wife died. At an early age, Mama learned to cook by the "dump method," measuring by sight and taste and feel. For many years she worked at her mother-in-law's tiny, take-out café, where Mama started learning the business side of the restaurant industry.

In 1976, she was ready to open her own restaurant. She had $64: $40 for food and $24 for change. The landlord of a closed, 18-seat café knew Mama was a great cook because of her already famous cakes and pies. He offered to let her start with no up-front deposits or rent "because he knew I didn't have any," Mama says. "He said to pay him when I could. It's a miracle."

Planning to open Mama Dip's Kitchen on a Monday, she was in the restaurant on Sunday fixing a meal for her eight children when a customer came in. Then another. And another. The morning's take was used to fund the lunch meal and the lunch profits financed the dinner. She made $135 that first day cooking eggs and grits, chicken and gravy, greens, and biscuits.

Fledgling business owners with no cash, credit, or financial backers must substitute hard work for capital. They do work themselves that well-heeled competitors would pay employees or outside contractors to do. Mama had just herself, but she was used to hard work going back to her childhood.

"I put in a lot of hours," Mama recalls. "At first I was open from seven in the morning to one the next morning because that's when other restaurants were open. I did it all myself for three years. My children would come to work after school and help me, but they needed to go home at night, so I'd close by myself."

Mama had just nine-and-a-half years of formal education, but after opening the restaurant she attended business classes and seminars to learn the best management skills. Eventually, she closed at 10:00 PM and in recent years started opening at 8:00 AM. Mama Dip's Kitchen became a Chapel Hill institution, attracting such customers as basketball great Michael Jordon, who played for the University of North Carolina Tar Heels, and the late *New York Times* food writer Craig Claiborne. In spite of her dump cooking methods, Mama wrote her own cookbook, *Mama Dip's Kitchen.*

"I never thought about the long hours," she says. "I came up in a culture where that's what everybody did. My mother died early and my father raised us. Our house was full of joy."

Today four of her children and two grandchildren work in Mama Dip's Kitchen. Mama still works every day, travels selling her cookbook, and is writing a second one.

"I don't do computers," she says. "I only have a pencil."

---

8. PERSONAL SAVINGS

The habit of saving money is important for the person
who wants to start a business and succeed.

■ ■ ■

When Gary Blinn served two tours of duty with the U.S. Navy in Vietnam during the 1960s, he saved 95 percent of his military pay. About all he spent was a dollar a week on cigarettes. The Navy paid for all meals, and he had few places to spend money on the Mekong River, so Gary put his pay into government savings accounts earning 10 percent interest. "The government encouraged saving," he says, dryly.

When Gary got out of the military, he used his savings to help finance his masters of business administration studies at Harvard University. Upon graduation, Gary went to work for the international banking division of the First National Bank of Chicago. He worked for ten years in Panama, Guatemala, Brazil, and Hong Kong, among other overseas assignments. During that time he and his wife saved half of his pay.

"My wife and I were both poor kids, so we learned to save," Gary says, adding that his employer would help with overseas expenses. "The bank would try to make up any differential in costs of living, such as the higher cost of air-conditioning in Saudi Arabia, so that employees would accept foreign assignments. They would compute what an apartment would cost in Chicago. Employees would pay that [amount], and the bank would pick up any additional cost of housing."

Gary didn't even own a car until he was 38.

His longtime habit of thrift gave him a large nest egg with which to buy Norfolk Beverage Co., a Budweiser distributor in Norfolk, Nebraska, when he left the bank and returned to the United States in 1982.

"Four years at Annapolis [U.S. Naval Academy] and eight years of active duty in the Navy taught me what I need versus what I want," Gary says. "When you have wonderful friends and good medical coverage, you don't need a great deal more."

It became easy for Gary not to spend every dime he made because he had cultivated an attitude of satisfaction with whatever he had. Equally important was to develop the habit of saving money at an early age and to stick with it consistently. By putting the money into savings accounts up front, it isn't missed as much as if it is the last payment made at the end of the month. For Gary, saving became second nature.

His discipline of saving is a model for all would-be business owners because virtually all of them must rely on savings, not just to buy or start a business, but to live on until the venture can afford to pay the owner a salary. Also, throughout the life of the business, the owner needs the discipline to save money for taxes, for unanticipated expenses such as broken equipment or accidents, and for growth opportunities. Gary and his wife continued their saving ways even as Norfolk Beverage Co. prospered.

"We paid cash for our house; our vacations are not expensive," Gary says. "I wanted to be an archeologist, so I like to go on digs to Roman forts in England, eat beans out of can. That's a lot more fun than fancy hotels."

9. USING JOBS TO FINANCE A DREAM

Many entrepreneurs work extra jobs to raise
the capital to start their businesses.

■ ■ ■

Beverly Stewart knew from the first grade that she was called to be in education and initially took a traditional path as a teacher, earning bachelor's and master's degrees in education and teaching in a public school.

"After five years I realized it was hard to reach every student, and that frustrated me," Beverly says. "I would tutor during recess and after school. I realized that to teach the way I wanted, I would have to do it one on one. One-on-one teaching is always successful."

That's when Beverly started working extra jobs to save money to start a tutoring service. She taught summer school. She sold toys and gifts through home parties. She ran a pet-sitting service "before it was popular," she laughs. And, of course, she started tutoring part time. In 1985, she opened Back to Basics Learning Dynamics at the kitchen table of her one-bedroom apartment in Wilmington, Delaware.

One of the characteristics of people who will be successful in business is hard work, even before the firm opens. They calculate their capital needs, cut personal spending, scrimp, and save. Beverly's willingness to work not just one but four extra jobs to raise capital made Back to Basics Learning Dynamics a reality sooner than if she worked one part-time job or tried to save out of her regular teaching salary. But the mind-set Beverly exhibited of putting her own money into her plan is widespread. Beverly was willing to step out of her educational training and take on work that others might not think of as long as it was legal and people would pay for it. She accepted humble jobs that less driven people might reject.

"I didn't want a loan; I never took one except for mortgages in the buildings the business bought," Beverly says. "We're very self-sufficient. I don't like debt."

Beverly also applied this work ethic to the business in its early years. If students couldn't come to her kitchen, she went to where the students were.

"We go to private homes, to schools, to offices for adult students," she says.

Just as she had to raise money to start her business, Beverly found that she had to earn business knowledge on the job. "I had never taken a business course. I had no background in business," she says. "I had a lot of common sense and knew how to treat customers right, but not having the background, it took me longer to get where I wanted to grow."

Since 1985, Back to Basics Learning Dynamics has tutored more than 8,000 students from Pennsylvania, Maryland, and Delaware. The company now has more than 100 tutors and is one of the largest companies in Delaware. It tutors students of all ages, employees under contract with corporations, and homeschoolers.

"You don't need to start off with a big building," Beverly says. "I've seen people try to start big and fail."

10. CAPITALIZE YOUR SCHTICK

An entertaining talent can help finance your real business.

■ ■ ■

Gary Roma has found a way to turn his lifelong love of puns and a knack for smart, stand-up comedy into capital for his real start-up business, Iron Frog Productions, a documentary film producer in Boston, Massachusetts.

Like many entrepreneurs, Gary uses whatever skills and experiences he has to further his long-term business goals. Eventually he hopes to be a full-time documentarian, but professional investors don't beat down the doors to finance such projects. That's when creative capitalization steps in.

"I started doing comedy in the early '90s at open-mike nights at clubs," Gary says. "I have a specialized routine that's on the literary side so I decided to find a niche at libraries, conferences, and MENSA [high-IQ society] meetings."

Gary's "literary" humor goes like this:

A consonant walks into a bar and sits down next to a vowel. "Hi!" he says. "Have you ever been here before?"
"Of cursive," she replies. "I come here, like, all the time."
He can tell from her accent (which is kind acute) that she is a Vowelly Girl.

Librarians love it.

So Gary uses it to finance his documentary film research. One of his documentary films, *Puss in Books*, is about cats that live in libraries. "There is actually a Library Cat Society, believe it or not," Gary says.

The documentary film won "best documentary" awards from a couple of film festivals and was screened at the National Gallery of Art in Washington D.C. and the Museum of Fine Arts in Boston, which boosted Gary's *bona fides* with meeting planners. So did his selection as Punster of the

Year in 2001 by the International Save the Pun Foundation (yes, there actually is such a group, based in Toronto, Canada). With these successes as testimonials, Gary turned *Puss in Books* into a means to raise capital for the next documentary film.

"I wrote a stand-up routine that included a library theme," Gary says. "I put together a 90-minute show in which I screen my films, present my routine, talk about my films, answer questions from the audience, screen clips from my upcoming film, and have a drawing to give away videos."

Gary presents this entertaining program for a fee to conferences and library associations, such as the New England States Touring Program and New Hampshire Library Association. When he started work on his new documentary, *Floss! A Meditation on the Possibility of Change*, he contacted libraries in locations that he needed to visit to film interviews.

"For example, I needed to do some interviews in upstate New York, so I booked four shows, Monday through Thursday nights in the area," Gary explains. "I had the days free to do the interviews for my documentary. The fees I was paid for my show along with money from video sales covered the cost and more of my trip."

This traveling pun-fest capitalizes his film making but not his living expenses. Gary works part-time for a market research firm in Boston, where his hours are flexible so that he can tour for his speaking and film-making projects.

11. SEVERANCE PAY

Extra payment from a corporate employer at the time
of layoff from a job can provide a sizable amount
of money to start a business.

■ ■ ■

When Rick Usher was laid off as a corporate attorney from a large oil company in 1993, he received two years' salary as severance pay. Initially he thought he would look for another corporate job, but the economy was slow and the job market woeful for his level of management job. So he sat down with another attorney and wrote a business plan for a new law firm, Furman Usher Inc., which is now in Irvine, California.

Corporate downsizing and layoffs have become a fact of American life. Even in good times, companies may eliminate jobs or close divisions or move as their strategies and fortunes change. Many offer extra compensation, usually based on years of service to the company, in addition to the final paycheck. Others, in lieu of outright layoffs, offer to buy out some employees in the form of a cash bonus, lump-sum payment of retirement plan benefits, some salary or health insurance continuation, service years added to retirement plan, or outplacement services to help find another line of work. In both cases, the extra cash usually comes with an agreement not to sue the corporate employer for wrongful termination, age or racial discrimination, or other issues. Most people who are laid off either get another job or retire, but 5 percent to 20 percent of them try their hand at entrepreneurship as Rick did.

"Having been through exposure to politics at the senior [management] level, I was tired of that side of corporate work, tired of the travel, and I wanted to control my own destiny," Rick says.

He was young enough that he believed he could return to the corporate world if he did not like running his own law practice. While the step wasn't risk-free, it was a relatively inexpensive gamble with a large upside.

"There was not a lot of capital expense in my start-up," he says. "As a professional in a service business I did need an office and all the accompanying expenses. I needed to do marketing, which for me, was primarily networking."

Although his initial money requirements for his law practice were modest, Rick knew he would need money for living expenses until he could gain enough clients. That's where his severance pay served its best purpose.

"You should have enough money to carry yourself for a year before you can expect your business to carry you," Rick says. "You should start generating revenue as you get going, but it won't be enough to cover all costs for a while."

Rick spent his first year in business developing a support network and a list of clients. Once he had the clients, the work was easy. It was the marketing that was new for the one-time employee of a large company.

"In the corporate world, you have someone else to do the tasks you don't like or you're not good at," he says. "In your own business, you must do them."

Rick's partner couldn't adapt to the self-employment life and eventually returned to a corporate job. Rick even flirted with the idea as the economy improved but decided he enjoyed serving and developing relationships with clients face-to-face without layers of bureaucracy. He learned to enjoy the freedom of being the boss and the satisfaction of self-accomplishment. A paycheck from another company only seems more secure, he reasons. Another layoff is always around the corner in twenty-first century business. But Rick is thankful to have received a head start from a severance package to ease into business ownership.

12. PAY AS YOU GO

Many types of ventures can finance the start-up phase
with revenues if new-business growth is modest.

■ ■ ■

Pam Lontos racked up hundreds of thousands of miles as a professional speaker on sales training and personal motivation. But after 18 years, she wanted to travel less.

"I got the idea to start a public relations firm out of the blue," Pam says. "I calculated that if I got one or two clients, I would only have to travel twice a week."

Pam called four friends who were also professional speakers seeking their advice about the feasibility of her idea. Three of the four said that if Pam opened a public relations consulting practice, they wanted to be clients because they knew how successful she had been getting publicity for herself as a speaker and author. The next day, Pam started PR/PR in Orlando, Florida. However, she didn't shut down her speaking business immediately. First, she had speaking commitments 18 months into the future. Second, the speaking income came in handy while building PR/PR. Within a few months, Pam had succeeded in getting articles in magazines about her initial three clients. When people asked how they had managed to get such coverage, they gave out PR/PR's phone number.

"A lot of times people think too much," Pam says. "I already knew how to do publicity; it was a matter of jumping in and doing it."

Many service businesses, like public relations, can start part-time with relatively little capital, especially for someone like Pam who already had an existing company with an office, equipment, staff, and most important, management experience. She could continue to use her speaking income to pay living expenses and put public relations revenues into growing the new business, buying equipment and databases she didn't have previously. Pam also shifted her time and spending on marketing away from attempts to attract new speaking engagements and shifted them toward seeking public relations clients. "The money I was putting into brochures, ads, and mailings for speaking, I reversed and put that into the public relations business," she says.

Within 12 months, Pam was doing public relations full-time and speaking became the side business. After another 6 months, she closed the speaking and training business completely. It was a gradual process that many people, who are eager to throw themselves into a new venture, won't follow, Pam says. One of her clients abruptly quit a $100,000 job to devote himself full-time to build his speaking business, "but he didn't have enough speaking jobs to warrant quitting his day job," Pam says. "It is possible to do both. Many speaking engagements are on weekends. The nice thing when you start small is that if you don't like it or it doesn't work out, you can get out without running up huge bills and have no income to pay them."

Pam has found that her public relations business can grow more quickly than her speaking business had because she can hire additional associates to handle all the clients she can attract. "When you're a speaker, you are the business and you can only do so many speeches," she says.

13. THE SUPPORTIVE SPOUSE

A working spouse who brings home a regular income
takes enormous pressure off a new entrepreneur
to turn a profit quickly.

■ ■ ■

Wendy Hager ran a small business in her garage while her daughters were young. But when her younger daughter entered high school in 1993, Wendy decided to start a full-time quilting shop outside the home. Wendy had a college degree in graphic design and had sewed for years. She also spent two years researching the quilting and retailing industries and writing a business plan. Still she had another advantage that greatly boosted the odds of success for Material Possessions in Lake Forest, California. Husband Jack's income as a mobile home designer covered all the family's living expenses.

"We didn't really have to sacrifice [at home], so everything I made in the store could go back into growing the business," Wendy says.

She didn't pay herself a salary for seven years. Material Possessions's sales were $350,000 the first year, doubled the second year, and have grown every year since.

Experts agree that an entrepreneur will have an extremely difficult time starting a business without the psychological and emotional support of the family, especially the spouse. But if that spouse is bringing home a regular paycheck, either from a job or an established and stable business, the entrepreneur has an enormous advantage. The new business can grow more slowly, and profits can be plowed back into the business at the least to keep it alive and at best to help it expand. In fact, the average new business doesn't turn a profit for 12 to 24 months. Trying to feed, clothe, and shelter a family during that time is tough.

The Hager family's needs were modest, which helped, Wendy says. And Jack never disparaged or doubted her business.

"He did question my choice of location in an industrial park," Wendy says, acknowledging that conventional wisdom says retailers must be in high-traffic, high-visibility commercial locations. "But a quilting store is a destination. We get customers from all over Southern California. When people from other states come here on vacation, they seek me out."

Wendy wasn't a quilter who wanted to expand a hobby into a business. Her research told her this was a burgeoning industry with a loyal customer base. "Quilting is a $2.2 billion industry with more than two million quilters in the United States," she says. "It also has a strong presence in Europe, New Zealand, Australia, Japan, and Canada."

Jack's early support for Material Possessions, which helped secure its long-term success, proved providential in 2001 when his own industry faced cutbacks, and he was forced into early retirement.

"Then the pressure was on me to meet our expenses," Wendy says. Fortunately, by that time Material Possessions was up to the task. The store has 14,000 customers, 30 employees, and 25 independent contractors who teach 150 different quilting and doll-making classes every three months. Wendy had developed the experience to know how much and when to order and the cash flow to weather seasonal fluctuations.

Jack's retirement freed him up to come to work at Material Possessions. He tracks inventory and logs new shipments.

"This is a difficult industry in which to manage cash flow," Wendy says. "I have nothing in August, and then the fabric manufacturers all ship at once, and I'm overwhelmed. Yet my customers are always looking for something new. I have 6,000 bolts of fabric, and they know which is new and which isn't."

14. PENSIONS

If a company pension allows distribution of funds
before retirement, the money can be used
for capital to start a business.

■ ■ ■

North Farms Cooperative had been selling organic and natural foods in Madison, Wisconsin, for 31 years when it went bankrupt in 2002. Seven of the co-op's former middle managers, each with a different operational expertise, got together to discuss the possibility of starting a similar distribution company. Organic retailing is a promising industry with U.S. sales growing 20 percent or more annually since 1994. Wisconsin, with more producers of organic food than all other states except California and Washington, is a good market for such an enterprise.

"The sales were there. The outlook was great. We just needed the money to get things going," says Kim Erdmann, general manager of the new company, Natural Farms Inc.

The new venture would be a for-profit distributor of natural and organic foods to grocers and health food stores throughout the Midwest.

"Why did we think we would make it when North Farm couldn't? In our minds, we, being middle managers, knew mistakes were being made [in the cooperative]. We were powerless to do anything but watch it fall. Its owners and top management really didn't understand the business setting."

The seven former coworkers believed so strongly in the company and their abilities that they pulled money out of their pensions to get the seed capital.

Some company pensions pay the total benefit in a lump sum when the employee leaves the business. Others have restrictions on or prohibitions against taking a distribution of funds before retirement. If the pension does allow distribution, the employee can roll the amount over into an individual retirement account or pay regular income tax on the amount withdrawn and spend or invest it any way he or she wants.

The seven partners of Natural Farms Inc. went to the bankruptcy court and paid $55,000 for the assets and intellectual property of their former employer North Farms Cooperative. Natural Farms bought the customer list; Web site and computer software to run it; North Farms brand, logo, and trademarks; and leftover inventory and supplies.

"The hard part was convincing the vendors to go with us," Kim says. "Some of them got burned pretty badly [by the failed cooperative]. So there was a lot of begging. Some gave us terms right away. Others wanted payment up front for a couple of times and then gave us terms."

At the same time that Natural Farms was reestablishing vendor relations, its partners contacted every former customer of North Farms to let them know about their new venture. Some of the customers were buying groups that pooled their money for bulk purchases to save 25 percent or more off of retail grocer prices. Some were willing to try Natural Farms, but others had already chosen other natural food distributors.

As Natural Farms established a firm foundation, its product line grew from 500 items to more than 2,600 products. Customers order over the Internet, by telephone, or from a catalog. Natural Farms's trucks or UPS deliver to customers in seven states, or customers can pick up their delivery at the Madison warehouse. Sales have grown from $300,000 in 2002 to $2.3 million in 2003.

15. ENTREPRENEUR ROLLOVER STOCK OWNERSHIP PLANS

This plan, approved by the Internal Revenue Service,
allows entrepreneurs to use pension money from
a previous employer to start or buy a business.

■ ■ ■

Derek Quinn had worked for several semiconductor companies for 26 years until forced into retirement by his last employer. Rather than settle into the front porch rocking chair, Derek and wife JoAnn decided to start a business in which they could work together. In 2003 they bought a franchise from V2K and opened under the name Orange County Interior Fashions, a Laguna Niguel, California, retailer of window coverings and carpet. But first they visited an attorney knowledgeable about Entrepreneur Rollover Stock Ownership Plans, ERSOPs for short.

Normally, if you are under 59½ years old and try to pull money out of a pension, 401(k) or 403(b) retirement plan, or individual retirement account you will pay penalties and income taxes totaling as much as 50 percent of the money withdrawn. The costs are so high that financial advisors rarely recommend using such capital to start or buy a business. However, the IRS has approved the ERSOP as a means to capitalize a business without penalties or taxes.

The ERSOP allows someone who has been laid off or has quit to invest pension money into building a company that will not just be a job but could fund the owner's retirement, which many small businesses fail to do. However, the plan must be structured and managed properly. Benefits specialists and attorneys can help.

In addition, it requires some confidence in your ability to run a successful business.

To establish the ERSOP, Derek created a regular C corporation (an S corporation doesn't qualify), Dr. Quinn Enterprises Inc. The corporation adopted a new retirement plan, and Derek rolled $100,000 from two former employers' retirement plans into this ERSOP account. Then he invested most of the ERSOP money in stock of Dr. Quinn Enterprises to launch Orange County Interior Fashions.

"It's a fairly straightforward process," Derek says. "We don't have to make payments as we would with a loan, so we don't have that pressure on our revenues. When the business is generating sufficient profit, we can re-fund the retirement monies used to start the business. If the business goes bankrupt, there is no [tax] penalty since there is no payback, but we lose our retirement funds."

Derek and JoAnn have their ERSOP administrator review the business each year to meet IRS requirements that the money has been invested in a valid business.

It's better to make one large investment, rather than transfer money from the ERSOP into the corporation as needed because every transfer costs $1,500 and requires a written explanation to the IRS, Derek says. "We want to be paying money back into the fund, not taking it out."

Retirement specialists charge fees of several thousand dollars to establish the ERSOP and to register it with the IRS, plus annual maintenance fees. However, these costs are less than the penalties and taxes that would have to be paid if the money were merely withdrawn from a pension or re-tirement plan. An ERSOP also costs less than most small business loans, even if a start-up firm could qualify for one. Even though the IRS has pre-approved ERSOPs in general, it's a good idea for the business to ask the IRS for an individual favorable determination letter for its own ERSOP to make sure it has been drawn up properly.

SECTION B

A LITTLE HELP FROM FAMILY, FRIENDS, AND COLLEAGUES

■ ■ ■

Sometimes a business just can't get started on the owner's bankroll. That's when you look around to relatives and acquaintances who know and trust you enough to make a loan or investment in the new venture. If people who know you won't give you capital, you are less likely to secure capital from strangers.

This capital need is a chicken-and-egg proposition. Which comes first, the relationship or the capital assistance? Most likely, successful entrepreneurs start with some relationships and get better at cultivating them in starting and growing a company.

16. FRIENDS AND FAMILY

Personal relationships are rich sources of business
capital, but communication must be clear to avoid
misunderstandings and long-term animosity.

■ ■ ■

Todd Rustman had years of experience managing investments, and David Gianulias had long experience in real estate when they teamed up to create GR Capital in Newport Beach, California, in 1995. The company bought foreclosed and dilapidated houses from the U.S. Housing and Urban Development, fixed them up, and resold them, typically within four months, at 30 percent to 50 percent profit. At social gatherings they talked about their business, and relatives and friends asked if they could invest in a real estate syndication to rehabilitate properties for quick turnover.

"Everyone saw that Dave and I were doing this," Todd says. "If you're a leader and inspire people, they want to know what you're doing."

Family and friends are among the most common sources of business capital, both for start-ups and ongoing ventures in the United States. These are people who know and trust you. If they won't put up their money, it is even less likely that strangers will. Especially for start-ups, expected interest rates or anticipated return on equity investment can be phenomenally high, Todd says. Family members, especially, can be sources of patient money.

For the first deal, Todd and Dave raised $120,000 from family and friends for one year with a guaranteed 20 percent return on investment. They bought seven properties in rundown neighborhoods, rehabilitated them, and sold each at a profit. GR Capital published a quarterly newsletter to keep investors informed about the work in progress. The deal closed on time and each investor made more than the guaranteed return. Since that first arrangement, some of these relatives and friends have participated in other deals, usually structured as limited liability companies (LLCs).

"LLCs are one of the easier ways for us to do investment protection and for keeping books and assigning costs," Todd explains.

It is important to remember that while these people are friends and relatives, the arrangement must be treated professionally with formal, written contracts so everyone understands the terms, promises, and risk, Todd says.

"Family and friends violate you more because they don't think you'll take them to court," he says. "One guy wanted out early, and the understanding is that in such cases the investor must find his replacement. He didn't, but we found another friend to come in to the deal. It did hurt the relationship a little.

"It is absolutely essential that we keep our word," Todd adds. "You have nothing if you lose your reputation."

If a company succeeds, it also gives family and friends opportunities they wouldn't have in many other investments. Dave's mother could have put her money in a savings account, but she believed in her son and invested in several projects, with different arrangements and returns, but always higher than a bank's offering.

The partners involved Dave's father in another company, Napa Wine Group and Levendi winery to produce premium cabernet sauvignon. The three could leverage relationships in California's wine country, pursue a different passion, and make money. But each partner understands the terms of the deal, the business, and the responsibility of each.

"Our first crush was 2001. We had 960 cases at $40 to $50 a bottle," Todd says. "It scared the dickens out of us when everyone said we made too much for a young winery. But we sold out."

17. INHERITANCE

A bequest from a relative or friend can make possible business start-up ideas that otherwise might never be tried.

■ ■ ■

Kristin Gillenwater and her husband were working at a software development company near Washington, D.C. Traffic was terrible. Housing prices were so high that they could afford only a small, older house. Kristin wanted to stay home with their two young children. The couple was miserable.

Then Kristin inherited some money from her father, who died of cancer. The sum, though not enormous, was enough to open a world of possibilities for the Gillenwater family. While on vacation in Virginia, they loved the area so much that they thought first that they would move to Roanoke and find jobs with less stress and a lifestyle more to their liking.

"But then we said, 'Let's find something we can do for ourselves,'" Kristin says.

They started looking through real estate magazines and saw an ad for Meadowood Bed and Breakfast in Meadows of Dan, Virginia, in the heart of the Blue Ridge Mountains. The inheritance more than covered the down payment for the 4,600-square-foot house and surrounding 20 acres of fields, forest, pond, and natural springs. There was enough money left over plus the profit they made from selling their Washington, D.C., home for living expenses until they could build up a clientele for the bed and breakfast. The previous owners had run Meadowood as a side business without much advertising or official records, so the Gillenwaters, who bought the property in 2004, started marketing and running it like a business.

The inheritance made self-employment and a complete lifestyle change possible for the Gillenwaters. Recipients cannot plan on such a gift, and many of those who receive an inheritance don't want to buy or start a business. It means foregoing other purchases that beneficiaries might want. Kristin was more reluctant than her husband to become an entrepreneur.

"I worried about getting health insurance, but I had to give up worrying and thinking about being taken care of by a corporation," she says. "You only live once and if I didn't take the risk given this opportunity, I'd kick myself later. It's good to try business ownership when you're young and able to work hard."

Fortunately for Kristin, she didn't have many competing dreams of trips or fancy cars for her inheritance money. The only wish on her list was a larger house, and she got more than she imagined with the bed and breakfast. So it was easy for her to resist the temptation to fritter away the inheritance or use it for living expenses. That discipline and what some would consider sacrifice is a key difference between those who successfully turn an inheritance into a business and those who don't.

"One good thing about the inheritance is that I didn't get the money right away," Kristin says. "It took two years because my father didn't have a will, so we had a lot of time to think it through. Some of the discussions my husband and I had were what we could do for a living."

The bed and breakfast not only suited the Gillenwaters's need for an income, but it matched their desire for a less stressful lifestyle and good place to raise children. This match makes the inheritance an even better investment.

"When I saw the ad for Meadowood, my husband said, 'Let's go for it.' But we had stayed at a bed and breakfast once and he hated it," she says. "What he hated was not being in control. Being the host is a lot different than being the guest."

18.

CONVERTIBLE
DEBENTURE BONDS

Wealthy individuals are often more willing to loan money
to a start-up company than to accept equity. Convertible
bonds can be a beneficial compromise.

■ ■ ■

Frank Shemanski had much of the money he needed to start Southwest Financial Services in Brea, California, in 1988. However, he sought
25 percent of the capital from family, friends, and wealthy professional associates from his days as an executive with financial institutions.

Frank only accepted money from people he knew, but even good
friends and Aunt Bertha aren't too crazy about taking stock in a start-up
company.

"It's always easier to get debt than equity to start a business," Frank
says. "When [an individual] loans your business money, even if you pay it
back, there are always issues about whether the interest rate should have
been higher or the money repaid sooner."

Such individual loans should have a written agreement spelling out the
terms and interest rate so there's no dispute later. Frank, with the help of
attorneys, created convertible debenture bonds for Southwest Financial
Services, which provides merchant credit card services to businesses
through banks. A debenture is a bond that pays interest and is backed by
the credit of the issuer but not by any specific collateral. The holder has
first call on the issuer's income and unpledged assets if the debenture isn't
repaid. Southwest Financial Services's debentures had an interest rate av-
eraging 12 percent, and they were convertible, meaning they could be exchanged for stock in Southwest Financial Services.

Debt is tough on a young company because repayment is mandatory
and steady, which can drain needed resources. "It's not a good idea, but
when you're a new company you don't have options," Frank says. He
wisely put four of his biggest debenture holders on his board of advisors.

Frank thought for a long time that he might eventually take Southwest
Financial Services public. So he explained to his debenture holders that
they could vastly increase their eventual return on investment by convert-

ing their bonds to stock at 50 cents a share. Southwest Financial Services was an S corporation, so it could have only a limited number of shareholders. This type of business at the time was going public at $7 or $8, which would have been vastly better than 12 percent interest on the bonds. "These people had known me for years and knew this was an opportunity to make more money," Frank says. Many bond holders converted to stock, which eased cash flow for Southwest Financial Services. Those who didn't were gradually paid off.

After a short time, Frank looked at competitors who had taken their companies public, paying 15 percent of the capital raised to underwriters and $600,000 annually to file mandatory reports with the Securities and Exchange Commission. He decided to keep Southwest Financial Services private, which left his stockholders without liquidity for their shares, whose book value was around 30 cents. Frank offered to buy back their stock at 50 cents a share. "I paid back millions of dollars over the years; no one ever lost a penny."

A few decided to hang on to their shares, anticipating a much higher return when Frank eventually sells the company. Southwest Financial Services has grown steadily over the years, has always been profitable, and processes $100 million in credit card purchases a month. It earns a percentage fee on each transaction.

19. FORMER COLLEAGUES

When seeking start-up capital, don't overlook
people you have worked with in the past.

■ ■ ■

Tony Annan had worked as an estimator and project manager for a general contractor, when he decided in 1999 to start his own construction company. He had about $25,000 in savings, pension funds, and proceeds from the sale of property. But when he wrote his business plan for Warwick Construction Inc. in Houston, Texas, his capital needs were much higher.

"I did not have any wealthy friends or family to call on, so off I went looking for start-up capital," Tony says. Lenders wanted too much collateral; venture capitalists wanted too much equity. It appeared that Tony would either have to scale back his plans significantly or give up his dream. Then two former coworkers who had started their own construction company called him about the death of a mutual acquaintance.

"After all the niceties and condolences, we briefly discussed my goal of starting a new company," Tony says. "I didn't think the chances of investment from them were real good because they owned a similar business. To my amazement, they showed interest."

The former co-owners exhibited a common entrepreneurial trait: The willingness to help others in small businesses. Having gone through start-up struggles, business owners usually will provide advice, references to professional help, and even contracts and cash. These men invested $25,000 each and helped provide the backing so Warwick Construction could obtain a $150,000 loan.

"The agreement was that when I paid the note off plus interest, I could buy the remaining stock so that I would be majority owner," Tony says. "That was great incentive for me. I paid it off within a year."

"There is a fine line between borrowing too little start-up and operating capital and borrowing too much," Tony says. "Borrowing too little will result in too much time and energy spent micromanaging accounts payable and accounts receivable. Borrowing too much will result in being micromanaged by your creditors."

The help from his former colleagues and other business owners was a revelation for Tony. When he announced his new business, many went beyond encouragement and gave him small projects to get started.

"They could see my desire, pride of ownership," Tony says. "I structured the company so well that they saw it was professional. I think it was easier to get jobs when I started than now."

That's probably an exaggeration. Warwick Construction has grown to about 59 employees and $40 million in annual revenues. It is licensed in every state and has done work from Puerto Rico to Hawaii. Warwick Construction specializes in retailers that have plans for multiple units. "If you want one building, we're not the right company; if you want 15 or more, we're for you," Tony says. The biggest client is Gap clothing stores.

To attract and keep such clients, Warwick Construction provides extraordinary, ongoing service. "We have to service them in times when no one else wants to deal with them, even a little bathroom remodel. That's the last thing a general contractor wants to do, but if we do it, clients recognize that we are maintaining our relationship with them and they reward that," Tony says.

Tony's original investors are still involved with the company as directors. The trio's relationship has grown over the years to involve not just construction for others but real estate development and other ventures.

20. PARTNERS

An individual who lacks enough start-up capital should consider
whether to bring in partners to invest money and expertise.

■ ■ ■

Wilson Alers for years had thought about starting his own event production and technical services company. He treated each project as a learning experience, learned from mistakes his employer made, and kept personal debt and expenses in check. In 1990, he and coworker Oscar Colom and childhood friend Jimmy Pabon pooled $70,000 to start Media Stage Inc. in Sunrise, Florida. The company provides a complete turnkey system of audio, video, lighting, and other services for business and entertainment events.

"Originally it was going to be several partners, but at the last minute, when it came to putting up money, the others backed off," Wilson says. "Oscar and I had the experience and were going to run the company. Jimmy owns a bar and restaurant in Puerto Rico and was a silent partner."

The trio did what many people do when they lack enough capital and business experience on their own. They form a partnership with each contributing some of the needed start-up capital. Such businesses are stronger if the partners contribute more than money and if the partners have a written agreement in advance to answer important questions such as how authority and profits will be divided among the partners. The Media Stage trio wrote a buy-sell agreement to specify how to break up the company in the event a partner dies or leaves, and a business plan to delineate responsibilities.

"I wanted Oscar specifically as my partner to contribute capital but also to bring something more to the party," Wilson says. "We needed people who knew what they were doing. I had been the general manager [at the previous employer] and Oscar was technical engineer."

They both agreed they would not take a salary for six months because they knew the importance of investing in equipment and people to run a quality meeting production service. They bought used equipment from a professional friend who told them to pay when they could.

"I knew going in that banks wouldn't help, especially in our industry," Wilson says. "There's a high mortality rate for companies and high cost of equipment that a year later is obsolete and worth nothing.

"Starting a business requires experience, know-how, and sacrifices," he adds. "Fortunately, we were successful enough that we could start drawing a salary after three months."

Media Stage attracted *Fortune* 500 companies, large trade associations, and well-known entertainment industry clients based on the partners' experience and contacts in the industry. These events attract from 500 to 10,000 attendees. Some are simple motivational sales meetings. Others require scenery, videos, live performers, and venue rental. Media Stage provides everything. The partners can draw on the skills of their 22 employees in Florida and five employees in Puerto Rico, plus freelancers across the country for specialized services.

"I've been doing this since 1979, so I have a bevy of engineers who travel with us around the world to create outstanding corporate events and support live performances," Wilson says.

"There is no downside to a partnership if you have the right partner," Wilson says. "We complement each other. I do sales, and Oscar does the technical side. We always consult each other about equipment and other major purchases, and we always have three months of revenue in savings for a rainy day."

21. CUSTOMERS

Ask the buyers of your products or services to pay up
front to help with cash flow in early years or tight times.

■ ■ ■

John Matig was a minority partner in a steel manufacturing company, but decided in 1999 that he needed to be the majority owner in order to run the business properly and ethically. That's when he teamed up with

John Godwin and Michael Hancock to start Frontier Steel Co. in Canons-burg, Pennsylvania, to distribute carbon, plate, and other steel products.

John Matig promoted his new company to fabricators, railroad manu-facturers, construction companies, and energy firms whose executives had known him for a quarter of a century in the steel industry. Quickly, Frontier Steel was selling $300,000 to $400,000 worth of product each month, which was a blessing, but also a potential cash-flow nightmare.

"Most of them were my friends who knew we were starting a new business and that we were lacking in capital until we could get a line of credit," John explains. "They were willing to pay in advance for product until we got established."

Steel is a commodity whose buyers are looking for good service and extra value. If they get it from a supplier, they will tend to remain loyal for years, John says. Service and value were what Frontier Steel Co. promised to deliver.

A company that can start with even a handful of customers has a strong start because its owner knows there is market demand for his products or services. If those customers are willing to pay cash up front instead of ex-pecting to pay 30 days or longer after receipt of the goods, that action can be the difference between success and failure. In some cases, customers urge an entrepreneur to start a business to supply product they can't get anywhere else. That occurs when a sole supplier goes out of business or drops a certain product line. More commonly, the new business owner rec-ognizes the benefit or unmet need before the customer does and makes that pitch to the buyer to initiate the relationship. Most fortunate are entrepre-neurs like John who have long-term relationships with targeted customers who are willing to place an order with a new company because of the trust built up over long years of experience.

"You have to have an open book policy with your customers," John says. "It was being honest with them in terms of our percentages and profit margins. It was start a business or die. Customers knew we were just feed-ing our families and trying to take care of employees.

"Also, they knew [paying in advance for steel deliveries] was tempo-rary, three to five months, until we could establish a credit line," John adds. "When we got the line of credit, they went back to normal payment terms."

The initial strong relationship with customers helped Frontier Steel weather an industry slump in the early 2000s. After starting primarily as a distributor, Frontier Steel shifted to about 60 percent of revenue from processing and manufacturing to add value to the product that customers wanted and were willing to pay for.

"That change really helped us survive," John says.

Responding to customer requests also helped Frontier Steel grow from two employees to 27 in five years and from an initial investment of $120,000 to $26 million in sales in 2004.

22. CREATE DEMAND IN ADVANCE

If customers strongly desire a product or service that is not available in the market, they may be sources of start-up capital for a business that will satisfy their wants.

■ ■ ■

Cherene Raphael had a master's degree in fine art and a teaching credential, yet taught art classes for free in elementary schools in Fullerton, California. That's how strongly the gallery artist believed in the importance of early art instruction and encouragement.

She and husband, John, talked for years about opening an art school for children. Instructors would nurture students' self-esteem along with their artistic ability. Only constructive feedback would be permitted. Structured lessons would be fun while teaching art skills.

Landlords, convinced such a school wouldn't be commercially successful, wouldn't even lease space to the Raphaels. The city, influenced by press coverage of a notorious child abuse scandal at a Southern California preschool, resisted issuing permits to a private school. There were additional hurdles. "If we had said we were going to tutor art, we would have been ok, but we said we wanted to start an art school, so there were a lot of requirements for parking, handicapped access, and on and on," John says.

After two years of persistence, the Raphaels won city approval and a lease on the second floor of a building, certainly not ideal for The Art House, the name they chose for the business.

Despite the skeptics, The Art House had 40 students on opening day in 1987. By the end of the first month, 90 students came regularly. By the end of the year, 200 students enrolled. They came from as far as 30 miles away.

"All the marketing Cherene had done over the years as a volunteer teaching art in the public schools brought customers immediately; we were in the black the first day," John says.

It helped that The Art House ran economically. The Raphaels furnished the space with used school equipment. John handled the books and business side of The Art House and Cherene was the only teacher initially. Their 12-year-old daughter was the receptionist.

The Raphaels tapped into the resources that emerge when entrepreneurs meet an unmet need. Most public elementary schools offered little or no art instruction, especially the high-quality instruction that an artist and teacher like Cherene provided. It is the rare business opportunity that enjoys the strong demand to which The Art House opened. Usually a handful of eager entrepreneurs leaps to capitalize on a void in the market. Often such opportunities come when a manufacturer drops a product line or a specialty store closes in a small town. The ability to respond to such an opportunity requires extensive knowledge of the customers—in The Art House's case, parents who write the checks not children who take the classes—and the lack of competition, which in this case was the result of public elementary schools cutting back on art instruction.

"When we opened business, the [public] school teachers and administrators would send us students," John says.

The neighborhood demographics were also important to The Art House's opening day success. Many wealthy Koreans were sending their children to Fullerton for a good education, and the Korean culture places great value on art, John says. "They brought gifts to my wife because she was an artist."

And they enrolled their children in The Art House from its inception. The tight-knit Korean-American community would pass out flyers for The Art House to new immigrants.

"There's an Art House Web site in Korean that I didn't create," John says.

The Art House has six part-time instructors and is looking at additional locations throughout Southern California. Competitors have sprung up, but The Art House leaped one start-up hurdle by tapping into demand before opening the business.

23. SUPPLIERS

The companies that provide raw materials and products may be
willing to wait for payment, which is like an interest-free loan.

■ ■ ■

Chuck Davis started CTI/Valueline in Huntington Beach, California, in 1985 with less than half the capital he thought he would need to be a success. His business supplies specialty papers and films to architects and engineers.

In order to get started, Chuck's main supplier—the company he used to work for—allowed him 60 days to pay invoices. "My old boss knew how tough it was to launch a business, and he also knew that my success meant more business for him," Chuck says. "In most cases, suppliers are companies or divisions that are much larger than your company. Consequently, they have already jumped through the hoops required by the banks to get credit lines that are larger than you could get. Why not make it a win-win situation?"

Many suppliers are not so generous with start-ups. They demand to be paid in advance for initial orders until the new business establishes a record of prompt payments and profitability. Chuck's relationship with his vendor was a definite boost. However, the extension of payment terms, often called trade credit, is as valuable as cash and better than using a loan or credit card because the supplier usually doesn't charge interest on the unpaid amount.

A formal loan was not an option anyway, Chuck says. Some of the supplier's other customers were competitors of CTI/Valueline. If they had discovered such a loan, it would have hurt the relationship between these other customers and the supplier. But offering Chuck attractive terms accomplished the same thing and benefited both him and the supplier because as CTI/Valueline grew, so did the supplier's sales.

Chuck has found through the years that suppliers are very reluctant to lower their prices, but tend to be willing to extend the length of time before they get paid, especially if the customer's company is growing.

The value of a longer payment time is significant, Chuck says. If a company must pay its vendors in 30 days, but its customers are paying in 35 to

50 days, the company will have to have capital to survive in the meantime. If it uses a line of credit or credit cards, interest payments will add to the cost of doing business, which will either require higher and less competitive prices or lower profit margin and less capital for growing the business.

A company seeking longer payment terms from a supplier needs to stress the prospect of providing a steady and growing stream of orders. It emphasizes how much it will buy over the years. The more evidence the company can provide that it has staying power and will buy large amounts of product over a long period, the greater the likelihood the supplier will be flexible in payment terms. Of course, that proof is easier for an established company.

This supplier's flexibility can take forms other than a longer payment time. Another of Chuck's early vendors had a strict volume discount policy that gave lower unit prices for larger orders. Chuck asked the vendor to give CTI/Valueline its lowest unit price even though it was buying lower volume.

"I told them their best price would make us more competitive in the market and that by doing so we would build up to the volume that would justify the pricing," Chuck says. "They gave it a try and by the end of six months, we had reached the volume discount amount and eventually we became their largest distributor in California for that product, again a win-win situation."

SECTION C

BORROWING OPTIONS

■ ■ ■

New business owners lament the difficulty they have getting loans. Financial institutions have a fiduciary responsibility to their depositors and investors not to make risky loans. They want collateral and experience to back a loan. That's why new business owners often have to pledge their own possessions to secure start-up loans. Some special lending programs may have easier qualifying standards, but they also have specific goals they want to meet, such as to get people off welfare or to create more jobs.

24. CREDIT CARDS

While credit cards are the easiest loans to get, they must be
used with discipline and caution to avoid financial problems.

■ ■ ■

After working in transportation and logistics for 11 years, Mike Jarrett and his wife, Diane, started PackShip USA in Orrville, Ohio, in 1998. That business specialized in packaging and shipping high-value products sold online, a service that was in its infancy at the time. Mike continued to work for FedEx Supply Chain Services for another year while Diane ran the company. In January 1999, Mike quit his job to join PackShip USA and within three months had started a second company, Jarrett Logistics Systems, as an outside supply chain manager for midsized companies throughout North America. Although the two companies are in different industries, they share headquarters and some administrative staff, which saves customers money.

During the start-up phase, Mike got some of his initial capital from credit cards, one of the most common sources of short-term business financing both for start-ups and more mature companies. Credit cards are relatively easy to obtain and provide convenience and simple tracking of expenses. On the down side, unfettered credit card buying can bankrupt a small business. Mike wanted to maximize the benefit and minimize the risk. He received numerous offers for credit cards with an introductory 0 percent interest rate. He signed up for several such cards, maximized their usage until the introductory rate ended, and then switched the balances to other zero-interest-rate cards.

"I could juggle those cards because I got credit solicitations all the time," he says. "It was cumbersome but it worked like interest-free loans."

Many business owners use similar methods when the credit card companies are competing for new business by offering low or no interest, usually for three to nine months. Some financial institutions offer incentives for transferring larger amounts, such as 1 percent interest on $1,000 balance but 0 percent for $5,000. Some institutions charge a fee to transfer the balance from another card. Any business owner who plays this game must keep good records or suddenly face a stiff regular interest rate once the introductory period is over. Some banks offer the enticing rates to win back customers who have dropped their credit card or haven't used it in a long time. Ironically, a business owner who transfers balances from one card to another improves the firm's credit rating because it is paying off large debts. However, if the owner overdoes it, the credit companies will ding his rating.

"I think at one time, I had two or three cards that had thousands of dollars' balance each," Mike says. "I have a pet peeve about paying interest. I was fully cognizant how much I had on each card and was fully committed to paying them off as soon as possible."

That attitude was not an idle boast. Mike and Diane paid off the mortgage on their first house in six years. Remember Mike's pet peeve. He didn't take that action to better position the family financially to start two businesses, but it certainly helped. "Some people are so burdened by debt that they can't make a career change. I didn't necessarily want to own a business, but I did want as much control over my destiny as possible."

In addition to discipline to keep track of credit card interest rates, a business owner should use the transfer practice only temporarily, Mike says. "Once both companies got on their feet, I paid that credit card debt off. I have no problem using credit and making it work for me, but not to the point it controls what I do."

25. SBA MICROLOANS

The U.S. Small Business Administration guarantees
small loans to new businesses made by nonprofit,
community-based lenders in every state.

■ ■ ■

Victor Valdez of Nogales, Arizona, hated struggling with trash bags whenever he raked leaves. So in 1996 in his garage he created two interlocking aluminum hoops that would hold the bag open. Victor initially named the product E-Z Bag Snap Ring but later changed it to BagWizard. Almost immediately his family and neighbors wanted Bag Snap Rings too, so Victor started a side business making them in a ten-by-ten-foot shed.

He even patented the product and started E-Z Bag Snap Ring LLC. But when he approached banks about a loan to develop the molds to start mass-producing the Bag Snap Rings, he was turned down.

"Nobody would loan to me," he says. "When you start something new with no market analysis or track record, people are very skeptical."

Then Victor saw a small story in his local newspaper about PPEP Microbusiness and Housing Development Co., which had several offices in southern Arizona including one in Nogales. PPEP was one of dozens of nonprofit, community-based organizations nationwide that the U.S. Small Business Administration has designated as intermediary lenders for the SBA's microloan program. These intermediaries provide technical assistance and loan as much as $35,000 at reasonable interest rates to newly established or growing small businesses. The loan terms and interest rates vary according to the amount borrowed and the planned use for the money, according to the SBA.

Traditional lenders, even with the SBA's guarantee, have shied away from start-ups and loans of less than $100,000, which are as time-consuming to make as large loans and less profitable. Yet fledgling entrepreneurs have created numerous innovations from airplanes to zippers. The microloan program is designed to encourage this entrepreneurship and innovation and help businesses with fewer than five employees, which account for more than 60 percent of U.S. companies according to the Census Bureau.

At first PPEP helped Victor learn how to conduct research and development for his product, its packaging, and his fledgling business. In 2000, PPEP loaned him $3,000 for working capital and to buy specialized equipment to make plastic prototypes of the BagWizard. The product is now made by an injection mold process.

As important as the money that PPEP provided was the assistance in writing a business plan. "A good business plan is a must; you have to have ten-year projections, which helps foresee anything that can happen," he says. The plan also helped attract some private investment.

After receiving 20 hours of technical assistance and business training, Victor was eligible for a $15,000 SBA-guaranteed microloan. He used that money to develop packaging and conduct more market studies and focus groups on product acceptance.

In 2002, BagWizard sales were $12,500 a month, and Victor obtained another $5,000 microloan to expand market share and attend the International Hardware Expo in Chicago.

"We have sold the product at home shows and on QVC television shopping network," Victor says. "Home Depot and other retailers are interested in stocking BagWizard."

Victor is now ready for nationwide and international shipping from production facilities in Hermosillo, Sonora, Mexico.

The microloan and technical support launched BagWizard, Victor says. PPEP "believed in my initial concept. They have seen me through the entire process, and they are still providing support on the big picture for my business."

26. ACCION MICROLOANS

Private loan programs are available to provide small
amounts of money for young firms and start-ups
that can't qualify for regular bank loans.

■ ■ ■

Juan Altamirano wanted to start importing Central American products to boost revenues at his small grocery store in Miami, Florida. He borrowed $6,000 from a loan shark who charged $100 a day in interest. Fortunately for the survival of his company, El Norteno Distributors, Juan found a more economical source of capital: ACCION USA, a private, nonprofit organization that makes small loans to business owners that can't qualify for traditional financing. ACCION's national headquarters is in Boston, Massachusetts, with offices in eight other states including Florida.

Juan borrowed $6,500, enough to pay off the loan shark and launch the food import and distribution business. The interest was $300 total.

"ACCION made it easy to apply, very quick," Juan says. "I had the money within two or three weeks."

The United States has an estimated 13.1 million owners of businesses with fewer than six employees. More than 80 percent have never borrowed from a bank for business. Such capital is especially hard to get for minorities, immigrants, women, and new businesses. These groups comprise ACCION's target market.

ACCION loans $300 to $25,000 for 3 to 48 months to first-time borrowers like Juan with interest rates around 10 percent to 16.5 percent. Once borrowers prove they can repay the first loan, they can borrow more. Juan was able to borrow $12,000 more for grocery store inventory and expansion of distribution.

"My whole family was involved when we started business in 2001," Juan says. "When I met the people from ACCION, I did the math and, of course, it was better. I could put the money into the business instead of pay a loan shark."

ACCION gets its money from large banks, which apply their investments toward mandatory community reinvestment credit, and from private foundations such as the Ford and McArthur foundations. From 1994 through 2003, ACCION disbursed more than $66 million in loans to 8,300 small-business owners.

ACCION is more like the farm club for traditional lenders rather than a competitor. If a businessperson can qualify for a regular loan, even those guaranteed by the U.S. Small Business Administration or agencies in various states, ACCION won't make the loan.

But ACCION doesn't give money away to just anyone who has a vague notion of starting a business, says President William Burrus. "Our borrowers are in business already or have made a substantial sweat equity investment to get one started. The more they demonstrate they are serious about it, the better it is for us."

Juan and his family are serious. His wife, Marjorie, prepares 25 different traditional Nicaraguan dishes. His father and brother work in the company too.

"We do whatever we have to to bring the people in and make money," Juan says. "For us to get the money back, to pay the rent and pay our four employees, it is really a struggle. We started El Norteno Distributors in hopes that it will be the real money maker."

Juan imports cheese from Columbia; cookies, crackers, and biscuits from Honduras; and bread from several different countries.

"I have to be smart, insist on quality standards, and lower my costs of transport," he says. "Our biggest goal is to go to Nicaragua to get products for import and get rid of the middlemen. We need to increase volume and perfect the distribution channels and routes."

27.

SPECIAL LENDING PROGRAMS

Many communities have nonprofit entities that provide
small loans and business training to help people
start and succeed in their own firms.

■ ■ ■

Shelly Robbins has wanted to own her own business since she participated in Junior Achievement in high school. In the mid-1990s, she started exploring how to turn her bookkeeping skills into a full-time business. She received a flyer for free business training classes through Washington CASH (Community Association for Self Help) and started attending to learn the nuts and bolts of setting up her own business. Pregnancy forced Shelly to drop out before finishing her training. But in December 1999, she finally opened The QuickSource, a bookkeeping, consulting, and Quick-Books financial software training service in Seattle, Washington.

Within a few months, her business survival was in jeopardy when the accountant who had bankrolled the business withdrew the money. Shelly was in contact with Washington CASH about teaching QuickBooks workshops to fledgling business owners and discovered the group's loan program that might save The QuickSource. Soon she received a $20,000 loan to buy out the departing partner and pay for equipment and QuickBooks certification.

"I'm positive a bank would never have loaned me $20,000," Shelly says. "I had no assets."

Many cities and states have nonprofit entities like Washington CASH that offer loans and technical assistance to help low-income people become self-sufficient by starting small businesses. Each program has different criteria and goals, but a small business owner can benefit greatly by meeting the standards.

In the case of Washington CASH, the lender gets its money for training and business loans from the U.S. Small Business Administration, banks, individuals, and foundations, such as the Hewlett-Packard Microenterprise Development Grant. It has trained 1,100 people and made 250 loans since its founding in 1996. While Shelly benefited from a more traditional loan program that requires applications and credit checks, Washington CASH has made most of its loans through its peer lending groups, fashioned after the Grameen Bank program in Bangladesh.

After completing Washington CASH's business training, graduates— mostly women—are assigned to a lending group of other women who want to start businesses. The group votes on each member's business loan, typically for just a few hundred dollars, and the entire group is responsible for the loan's repayment. Peer support for success and responsible behavior is strong. The program's foundation is "discipline, dignity, responsibility, courage, accountability, unity, and hard work."

"I didn't have the benefit of a peer group, but I teach classes there now and see how they help each other and push each other," Shelly says. "I definitely recommend the program, especially training to start a business. If you do the homework you will develop a business plan, which is critical."

Since receiving the Washington CASH loan, Shelly's business has helped more than 300 small businesses to grow and be successful. The QuickSource has seven employees and is adding more jobs and clients all the time.

"Many of our clients started their businesses because they have a skill or service or product that they believe will help others," Shelly says. "It is very gratifying to watch their businesses grow knowing that we are pivotal to their success."

28.   START-UP LINE OF CREDIT

A systematic search, good industry relationships, and
a strong business plan can uncover a lender willing
to extend a line of credit to a new company.

■ ■ ■

Vince Colarelli was one of the top executives at a large construction company in Colorado Springs, Colorado. But he wanted to create a company culture of personal accountability by each employee for excellent work and service for clients. It was easier to do that by starting his own company, Colarelli Construction Inc., from scratch than by trying to change a large corporation.

He started with a strong business plan for a general commercial contractor providing a broader range of services than most contractors, from design to construction management to facilities maintenance. He decided to build a strong, professional staff with long experience and a passion to do more than make a buck. The company's philosophy is that business is personal and relationships affect customers' buying decisions. Each employee is personally accountable for the company's performance.

Next he leveraged his relationships in the community and industry. Many areas have a tight-knit community of bankers, real estate people, estimators, and companies who know everyone and whether they are creditworthy. Vince approached 11 banks, from small community institutions to business banks.

"My strategy was trying to understand what the loan officer's perspective might be when considering a line of credit," Vince says. "I realized early on that community banks would be more restrictive. They don't have large enough assets for our needs. I aligned with a business bank that was fairly new that had a strong interest in the real estate industry."

The plan, the relationships, and the willingness to satisfy the lender's requirements earned Colarelli Construction a $300,000 start-up line of credit. Vince chose not to do business with some of the banks he approached, but none of them turned him down. Later, Vince added a $1 million line of credit from another bank. But the company has never had to touch either line of credit.

A strong business plan was only part of these bankers' willingness to work with Colarelli Construction. They consistently commented on the strong industry background of Vince and his team. "They said, 'We know your reputation,'" Vince says. "Our approach to business was something they believed in and they wanted to support."

In his first year in business, Vince signed $20 million in construction contracts including two major projects for Woodmen Valley Chapel, a large church in northern Colorado Springs. Colarelli Construction has also built banks, health facilities, and government and aerospace buildings. Vince's business plan that impressed so many bankers didn't project $20 million in annual revenues until Colarelli Construction's sixth year in business.

"We don't focus on our bottom line; we focus on serving the client," Vince says. "We're willing to lose money on a project if necessary to serve the client."

Vince even helped one client start up its own construction company because it was in that client's best interest to do its own building instead of using Colarelli Construction or any other outside firm.

"This industry tends to be short term," Vince says. "I'm a believer in the long term. I get a lot of repeat business."

29. STATE LOAN PROGRAMS

Each state has special programs that provide capital for
companies that meet targeted public interest goals.

■ ■ ■

Stephen Steed's family has been employed in the lumber industry for six generations. When Steve's employer, the lumber mill in Escalante, Utah, wanted to sell or close in 2000, he asked various government agencies whether they could help him and four of his relatives buy the company. Escalante is a town of 900 near Bryce Canyon, so the loss of a major employer was significant, but the closure of the mill would affect several counties in rural, southern Utah as well. It also would impact efforts to protect the national forests in the area. The U.S. Small Business Administration, U.S. Forest Service, National Fire Plan, Utah Rural Development Council, Utah Industrial Assistance Fund, and local Association of Government all had an interest in keeping the company open.

"They wanted business to stimulate the economy so they were willing to help with the seed money to get Skyline Forest Resources established," Steve says. "To qualify, Skyline had to create 50 jobs."

Skyline Forest Resources not only provides the required direct jobs, but its operations indirectly have created or saved many other jobs in the area. It is one of the largest private employers in southern Utah.

The government agencies' representatives did some creative thinking about various loan and grant programs available to help Steve save Skyline Forest Resources. The company had equipment to cut large-diameter logs, but the Forest Service told Steve that Skyline Forest Resources would be getting far more logs of nine-inch diameter or less. The larger mills would be inefficient in cutting smaller logs. The Utah Rural Development Council applied for and received a grant from the National Fire Plan. And then the council loaned the money interest-free to Skyline Forest Resources to help the company buy a $250,000 small-diameter log mill. The cooperative effort managed to get a good deal on the machinery and helped Skyline Forest Resources operate efficiently and make the most of every dollar it made. These rural companies always struggle to compete with larger companies. The Rural Development Council's interest is not to play favorites with rural companies or just boost local jobs, says Executive Director Scott Truman. The council works for healthy forests and watershed, two things helped by mills like Skyline Forest Resources.

Government agencies sometimes take a long time to make decisions or process the necessary paperwork. Steve worked most of 2000 and 2001 to get the support needed to start Skyline Forest Resources. The mill was closed for about six months.

"It was a matter of timing," Steve says. "We had been working with the state, and the Forest Service had a pilot project. No one had done anything quite like this before."

The company now mills pine, spruce, and fir into industrial house logs, construction lumber, and a specialty external siding. It markets its wood products through Teton West Lumber Inc. in Cheyenne, Wyoming, to retailers, builders, and other customers primarily west of the Mississippi River.

"We've gotten creative in what we're doing with marketing," Steve says. "We're always looking for ways to enhance value of the products we make."

30. SELLER FINANCING

In the purchase of a private company, the
seller often provides some of the financing.

■ ■ ■

In the early 1980s, the trucking industry was struggling with the impact of federal deregulation and a poor economy. The owner of a ten-employee repair shop for truck trailers in St. Charles, Missouri, wanted to sell the business, but not only couldn't get a good price, he could not find a buyer at all. Joe Helmsing, who had worked for the seller many years, decided this was the time to fulfill his lifelong dream of business ownership. So he stepped in to buy Craftsmen Industries Inc. in 1982. Although some people told Joe that the tiny repair shop could not be saved, "I thought I could turn it around," he explains. "I knew the company had some skilled people, and I believed we could do more with this business than just repair trailers."

Because the seller couldn't get any other deal, he provided the financing for Joe to buy the company—primarily its inventory—for $50,000.

The majority of small, private businesses cannot be sold when the owner wants to leave or retire. It is common, therefore, for the seller to take back a note to help finance all or part of the sale. One advantage is that it gives the buyer some reassurance that the sellers believe that the business can thrive without them. A bigger reason for seller financing is that the deal wouldn't happen without it. Most banks have strict lending criteria for business acquisition loans. The seller can accept more lenient qualification standards for the buyer than a bank would and a more flexible payment schedule, interest rate, loan period, and other terms. Some sellers will protect their continued investment in a company they no longer control by requiring the buyer to take out a life insurance policy with the seller as the beneficiary. Most sellers do not want to be tied to their former companies for many years, so seller financing is usually for seven years or less. Such a deal might be structured with a balloon payment at the end, paid by a new loan after the new owner has built a successful track record and financials to show a lending institution.

In the case of Craftsmen Industries, Joe paid off the seller in the second year of running the company. He was able to turn the small business around, "but it took a long time; no one wanted to hear my story for 15 years," he says.

Joe's strategy was to expand Craftsmen Industries beyond its trailer repair roots. The company began painting trailers as well as repairing them. Then it began designing and building specialty trailers, including the Oscar Meyer Wienermobile and the Sony PlayStation touring trailer. Craftsmen Industries added mobile display units, vehicle graphics, banners, and signs to its list of products. It started selling and servicing new and used trailers. It now sells more than 1,500 trailers a year, accounting for a third of its business. The payroll has grown to 215 employees.

"I believe you must continue to drive and push the company to grow," Joe says. "I don't want all my eggs in one basket, whether it is with one customer, one product, or one area."

31. FRANCHISE FINANCING

Some franchising companies will provide loans
to help people buy a franchise or equipment.

■ ■ ■

To become a business owner, Dave Potocki bought Spencer's Chem-Dry, a Glendale, Arizona, carpet and upholstery cleaning franchise in 1993.

Harris Research of West Logan, Utah, which has been franchising Chem-Dry since 1978, is one of dozens of franchising companies that provide financing for buyers of their franchises. Chem-Dry offers several different programs, depending on the purchase, says Franchise Administrator De Ann Corbell. In one common offering, Chem-Dry will carry back $13,000 of the $19,950 total investment at 5 percent simple interest to be paid back over five years. The company also gives franchisees a $500 rebate when they complete the mandatory five days of technical and managerial training before the franchise opens. Loan payments don't start for a few months, which helps the franchisee get started and earn some income first.

The idea to offer franchisee financing comes from founder Robert Harris, who worked his way through law school as a carpet cleaner. "The Chem-Dry system has made a new way of life and a new beginning for thousands of people," he says on the company Web site. The financing is obviously a good selling point. Chem-Dry has 2,500 franchisees throughout the United States and most take advantage of the program, De Ann says. Financing is not offered to overseas franchises. Instead, Chem-Dry sells territories to master franchisees, which in turn sell individual franchises under the master's own terms and conditions.

However, Dave couldn't use Chem-Dry's financing program in 1993. He was buying an existing franchise, and Chem-Dry only helps finance new franchises. But he did take advantage of the financing help when he bought a second franchise, Classic Chem-Dry in Buckeye, Arizona.

"The financing helps get started," Dave says.

Franchisors have a vested interest in providing financial help to potential franchise buyers. It can provide a competitive advantage. However, not every franchisor offers financial help to buy a franchise or required equipment. You should investigate before planning your future based on the hope that the particular franchise you want to buy comes with financing help. Furthermore, some franchisors that do offer loans may not provide interest rates or terms that are advantageous to the buyer. Do your research to find out if other loans with better rates are available from independent lenders.

Most, including Chem-Dry, do not finance the entire cost of starting the franchise. They set a minimum down payment price because they want their franchisees to have a personal investment in the business. A franchisee with no financial stake in the business has less reason to work hard to build success and more reason to walk away when the going gets tough.

Dave, with a background in marketing, says ownership, whether of a franchise or independent business, requires significant commitment and hard work. He has two employees, but still works 40 to 70 hours a week.

"I do a lot of the work myself, but I don't have stress, and I don't have to wear a suit and tie to work," Dave says.

SECTION D

OUTSIDE EQUITY INVESTORS

■ ■ ■

Professional investors who are not your family or friends might be willing to invest in a start-up company if the potential payback and ownership share are big enough. Such investors are not altruistic. They expect to be paid, just as lenders do. The less likely a business will make money, the less likely the professionals will be interested in owning a piece of it.

32.   MENTORS

Cultivate professionals and experts long before
starting a business. They can provide encouragement,
information, networking referrals, and capital.

■ ■ ■

When Kevin Maloney was a youngster, his mother worked in the
super computer division of California Institute of Technology, a world-re-
nowned science university in Pasadena, California. Scientists and engineers were always around Kevin's house. He even washed their cars.
Kevin listened to their discussions about research in such futuristic areas
as nanotechnology. Throughout high school and college, Kevin kept these
mentors up to date with his education and career.

"Every few years I'd send notes—'I'm off to grad school.' 'I'm starting a business.'—I was pleasantly aggressive," Kevin recalls. "Business
comes down to relationships, how you relate to people. I have always networked. I'm happily surprised so many people are willing to help young
people. It comes down to personality and persistence."

After earning an MBA from Pepperdine University in Malibu, California, receiving two patents for his invention, and working in several investment and capital management companies, Kevin became chief executive
at Quantum Sphere, a fledgling nanotechnology company in Costa Mesa,
California. This industry works with nanos, which are three to five atoms
in length. A human hair is 100,000 times thicker. Materials made that small
have different properties than their supersized versions, conjuring amazing
images of the information from millions of books being stored on a device
the size of a sugar cube.

But Quantum Sphere wasn't concentrating on those future promises
but rather on practical products that could turn a profit quickly, such as zinc
oxide nanopowder for cosmetics.

Kevin took his plans to a couple of his mentors, Marc Goroff and Jon
Faiz Kayyem, both PhDs from Cal Tech and founders of separate technology companies.

"I didn't ask for money. I asked for direction and advice," Kevin says. "They were so willing to share information and excited about my ambitious plans. After a couple of hours of conversation, they said, 'How can we get involved in this?'"

They listened because they knew and liked Kevin, but they asked about investing because his concept was strong. Although Kevin is a pleasant and intelligent man with a good resume, that goes only so far with mentors. They're more willing to part with advice than money.

"You can't just be a nice guy," Kevin says. "You have to have a solid plan, a solid business."

Faiz says he put money into Quantum Sphere because "it wasn't focused on 'stake your turf,' 'own your space,' and a quick IPO [initial public offering]. Others in nanotechnology talk about fanciful ideas that might not come to pass. Quantum Sphere knows there's a market for these particles [it manufactures] and passed its first [goals] early."

Faiz also is impressed with how closely Quantum Sphere watches its budget. It bought $76,000 in equipment for $4,000 at a bankruptcy sale. The company used its initial investment to build a reactor to produce nanoproducts at a profit before a couple of its venture-backed competitors.

In the late 1990s, technology companies could raise tens of millions of dollars from venture capitalists and go public without generating any revenue related to actual products. That era ended with the dot-com crash and is unlikely to return anytime soon. Instead, companies like Quantum Sphere are growing with fiscal discipline and the strength of relationships with mentors and other equity investors.

"We're positioning ourselves as a nano manufacturer that actually delivers products," Kevin says.

33. OUTSIDE INVESTORS

The payoff for nonfamily members willing to invest in a
new venture can run the gamut from high return on
investment to more work for investors' companies.

■ ■ ■

As a pediatric nurse, Sheree Mitchell saw a great need for a quality
child development center in her hometown of Columbus, Georgia. So in
1988 she quit her nursing job to build and open The Growing Room Child
Development Center. The start-up cost was $1.2 million.

"When most people hear you're going to start a child care center they
think you're starting in your house. We started in a 12,500-square-foot
building that we owned," Sheree says, adding with a laugh, "I said, 'If
we're going to go down, we're going to go down big.'"

She and her husband scraped together every bit of money they could
because they wanted to own controlling interest in The Growing Room.
But they gave up some equity to private investors in order to raise the capital for the 20 percent down payment for a government guaranteed real estate loan.

"These weren't friends. They were local businesspeople who had a lot
of faith in me," Sheree says. "I grew up in Columbus. The community isn't
that big [186,000 people]. Everybody knows everybody."

Some of the outside investors were involved in constructing the first
Growing Room child care center, she adds. They calculated that they would
get some of their investment back by participating in building the project.
Nevertheless, Sheree asked her attorneys to draw up a prospectus of The
Growing Room as a company worthy of investment.

Once an entrepreneur decides to seek outside equity capital, the business stakes rise significantly. The company must have a quality business
plan, good management experience, and reasonable expectation not just of
survival but also of big success. Equity investors aren't putting up cash for
altruistic reasons. They might accept more modest return on investment if
they see a civic need, as Columbus had for a quality child care center, but

they still expect a profit. Often these equity investors come from the ranks of suppliers, as they did for The Growing Room, or complementary businesses that have a natural working relationship with the new venture. But anytime you're giving up some equity in your business, hire an experienced business attorney to draw up and review all documents.

Even though Sheree had never owned a business before, she could capitalize on her experience as a registered nurse and pediatric specialist. She had an impressive business plan and could tell investors precisely how she would use their money to start and grow The Growing Room. Any start-up going after other people's money must provide more concrete facts about their ventures than the firm financed by the founder alone. However, that level of detail benefits a new owner like Sheree who lacks actual management experience.

Sheree's assessment of the market was accurate. The first Growing Room opened in August 1989 with 221 children. In 1996, Growing Room Too opened. In 2002, supplemental insurance company Aflac Inc., one of the city's largest employers, contracted with The Growing Room to run its two corporate child care centers. The Growing Room's staff doubled in one weekend with that expansion. In 2004, Cascade Hills Church contracted with The Growing Room to refurbish and run its child care center, expanding Growing Room's total staff close to 200 and enrollment to 1,300 children.

34. A MONEY-WANTED AD

You don't have to be high-tech, high-growth to attract investors,
but the search may be lengthy and serendipitous.

■ ■ ■

Like many entrepreneurs who hate to see a good product die, Diane Fallon was dismayed when her employer, a small-time book publisher in Irvine, California, decided to close with a book, *What to Do When a Loved One Dies*, still in the works. Her disappointment wasn't just the fact that she was out of a job. Diane had shepherded the book to the brink of publication.

"I believed in that book," she recalls. "I thought it would be a great seller."

Diane wasn't naïve. She had published books before and had been a consultant for other small publishing houses. In the latter capacity, she had even turned away clients because their dreams of profits were so unrealistic that she thought it cruel to give them false hope. Yet the vast majority of the estimated 10,000 independent publishers in the United States finds a specific niche and publishes three to five titles a year. These books typically are moneymakers if their subject matter is timeless, allowing sales over many years. *What to Do When a Loved One Dies* was just such an evergreen with potential bulk sales to funeral homes and estate attorneys.

Diane wanted to buy her former employer if she could raise the capital. Book publishing, like most industries, will not raise an eyebrow in venture capitalists' offices. But like restaurants, publishing has cache that attracts high-wealth individuals who love food or books. Finding them, however, is challenging.

Rather than thumb through the directories of venture capitalists, Diane placed an advertisement for a financial backer in *Publishers Weekly*, an industry trade magazine. She calculated that it was a publication likely to be read by book lovers and industry experts who just might know the right investor. Such capital searches are most successful when the marketing is targeted. The better you define your most likely investors and what they read or where they hang out, the more likely you will find the money you seek.

The ad brought several responses. The most promising call came from a retired attorney in New Jersey. She put together a proposal, based on her industry background and the death book's potential, and sent it by overnight mail to the potential investor.

He called and was interested, but was leaving the next day for Norway. The selling publisher wanted to close the deal quickly for bookkeeping reasons. Over the next ten days, Diane and her potential investor negotiated by fax. She asked for $50,000, $15,000 of which would buy rights to *What to Do When a Loved One Dies.* The investor was willing, but wanted to invest only for one year. The book wouldn't even be in stores for seven more months and distributors usually do not pay any sooner than 60 days after delivery. Diane managed to extend the contract. Then the investor wanted 75 percent of revenues; Diane talked him down to 60 percent.

"I had never had an investor before; I was clueless," Diane admits.

The deal was struck halfway around the world. Diane called her new company, Dickens Press, and *What to Do When a Loved One Dies* was its first project, selling about 10,000 copies.

35. ANGEL INVESTORS

High-wealth, professional investors are a source of capital
and advice for some early-stage, high-growth firms.

■ ■ ■

Brian Uffelman spent five years learning the real estate mortgage industry while working for someone else. He also identified a way to use the Internet to automate and improve service to lenders. Brian left his job in 1999 and honored his agreement not to compete with his former employer for a year. During that time, he wrote the business plan for iMortgage Services in Pittsburgh, Pennsylvania, to manage a nationwide network of appraisal and title companies to which lenders outsource these specialized activities.

"We started in April 2000, which was a good time for real estate and right before the Internet bubble burst," Brian says.

Brian's experience was in sales and marketing. He partnered with Shawn McCall, who had a master's degree in finance and a background as a corporate officer. They put together a solid management team and started shopping their business plan to the professional investment community. Most major cities have some high-wealth individuals who meet the Securities and Exchange Commission's definition of financially sophisticated investors who do not require the protection of special hand-holding when buying an equity position in a company. These investors are often called angels, but they're more like Dutch uncles, described by *Webster's New World Dictionary* as those who bluntly and sternly lecture and scold. Their investments often come with hands-on advice in day-to-day operations. Angels often have experience building successful businesses and like to invest in industries with which they are familiar.

Typically entrepreneurs like Brian meet angel investors through networking with gatekeepers such as accountants and attorneys. Although many angels prefer to remain virtually unknown, some actively participate in events and organizations designed to link entrepreneurs and capital investors. Angels also have invaluable business contacts. "One of the people I sent our business plan was not interested, but he forwarded it to someone else who knew more about the industry," Brian says. "That individual spearheaded a group of investors."

In the world of corporate fundraising, angels provide a bridge between investment from a young company's owners, family, and friends, and the venture capital funds. These venture capitalists provide larger investment but require the firm to be at a later stage of development. In iMortgage's case, the angels invested $290,000.

The company had to have a solid business plan, Brian says, but the angels were investing in the management team as much as in the plan.

The angels that invested in iMortgage have been relatively hands off about their investment, Brian says, which has both good and bad aspects. The management team has a freer hand to shape and grow the company. "But I muddled through some things that if I had more active investors might have gone smoother," he says.

For iMortgage, the Internet is merely the method for managing 7,000 vendors in all 50 states who provide financial institutions the services they need—from title insurance to flood certification—quickly and reliably. The Internet is an efficient tool, not an end in itself, Brian stresses. In spite of the Internet slowdown, iMortgage has $12 million in revenues and is aiming toward $50 million within five years.

The company is fortunate with its angel investors in another way. During the Internet bubble, angels often wanted their return on investments in two years or less, but in recent years they have become more patient. Brian says iMortgage bought out two of its angels, but the rest have converted their preferred shares into regular stock and are committed to the company long term.

"We have talked to venture capitalists, but our goal from the beginning has been to grow with cash flow," he says.

36. ANGEL CLUBS

Entrepreneurs can reach a large number of professional
investors in one presentation through the growing
number of angel organizations.

■ ■ ■

Thomas Lane owned a successful investment advisory company, but his first career was police officer and detective in Long Beach, New York, in the 1970s. That law enforcement experience taught Tom that police departments have a problem handling and getting rid of unclaimed confiscated property. With the rise of the Internet in the late 1990s, he thought it could be an ideal vehicle for bringing efficiency to the operation of police auctions, so he started Property Bureau in San Clemente. The company sells the confiscated property through Internet auctions, earns a fee and gives the rest to the police department. Tom's management team includes a technology expert, a former chief executive of entrepreneurial firms, and the former police chief of the Los Angeles Police Department.

For initial seed capital, Tom sought out individual investors, but the fourth time, he approached the Tech Coast Angels, a club of about 200 wealthy, professional investors with chapters in Orange, San Diego, and Los Angeles counties in Southern California. Financial angels have been an important source of capital for new and growing businesses in the United States for a long time. In recent years, these angels have been gathering into official groups. The United States and Canada had 50 angel groups in 1997 and 170 in 2002, according to the Ewing Marion Kauffman Foundation, which encourages entrepreneurship and sponsors the nationwide Angel Capital Association.

Each angel group has its own criteria. Tech Coast Angels look for early-stage technology companies in Southern California with market opportunity large enough to support a company with $50 million to $100 million in annual revenues, strong management, proprietary technology, and compelling strategy for capturing market share. These angels want to play a coaching and advising role with the companies in which they invest. The club doesn't invest in companies; individual members make their own investment decisions. Tech Coast Angels prescreen about 50 firms each month. About 20 get an opportunity to make a presentation to a screening committee. The best two make presentations to dinner meetings before the entire membership.

Tom was invited to make presentations to all three chapters, and more than 30 members eventually made investments in Property Bureau, totaling more than $1 million.

"It's an efficient way to raise money because you reach a lot of investors with one presentation rather than making 30 or 40 individual presentations," he says. "You have to prove your business model to get any funding. They ask hard, biting questions. You'd better know your business."

Property Bureau was appealing to members of Tech Coast Angels because it had revenues not just ideas, 150,000 registered users on its Web site, and hundreds of contracts with police agencies across the country.

"We're not really an Internet company; we're a service company," Tom says. "We take care of police departments' problems handling, maintaining, and moving property and turn it into cash."

Property Bureau also had a member of Tech Coast Angels on the management team, which gave the company validation as an entity worthy of a closer look. However, because individual money is on the line, these angels invest in opportunity, not friendship.

The Tech Coast Angels money helped Property Bureau grow 60 percent in a year. It has warehouses in New York, California, and Florida and anticipates 9 to 12 more across the nation. It is working to capture even more of the police market and expand to fundraising events for schools and charitable organizations.

"It's an easy way for parents to raise money for their schools," Tom says. "They clean out their garages. We sell the merchandise and give the money to the school."

37. LOOK FOR SYNERGIES

Large companies that can gain strategically from your
company's products or services may be sources
of early capital or growth capital.

■ ■ ■

When Paul Binsfeld's two-year-old daughter ran a high fever on a Friday night, he and his wife couldn't reach their doctor or anyone from their insurance company about the potential danger and whether the toddler needed to go to the emergency room. Paul, who worked in the insurance industry, thought insurers could benefit by providing their clients with 24-hour access to medical information that would handle such situations more quickly, efficiently, and accurately. And then he started thinking about other applications for such a service, such as immediate information for workers injured on the job. Instant first-aid advice, around-the-clock telephone availability of registered nurses, and immediate delivery of detailed reports could help workers get proper treatment sooner and speed their recovery. Swift action could help employers control workers compensation insurance costs.

Paul wrote a business plan in 1996 and started Company Nurse LLC in Scottsdale, Arizona, in 1997 to be the on-call nurse for hundreds of companies nationwide. The man in charge of mergers and acquisitions for Tenet Healthcare Corporation in Santa Barbara, California, knew Paul and introduced him to Tenet officials. The hospital giant was buying hospitals in Arizona and saw Company Nurse as a means to provide work to its medical facilities and doctors through patient referrals. Tenet invested $300,000 seed capital to help Company Nurse LLC get off the ground. The deal was a 50-50 joint venture to develop the concept in Arizona. Paul retained the right to develop the program independently in the rest of the United States.

"You might say it was a synergistic fundraising approach," Paul says.

Such strategic alliances can be a good source of capital for a young company that has a strong concept or intellectual property compatible with the interests of a major corporation. Especially in such fields as technology and health care, big corporations often decide it is quicker and cheaper to create a joint venture with a start-up than to develop the product or service on their own. Such ventures usually depend on the entrepreneurial company having relationships with professionals, such as attorneys or officers in the large corporation to help make the match. The giants are bombarded by so many offers that their officers rely on people they know and trust to separate the ideas worth pursuing from those that won't pan out.

The young company must also be alert to the potential for strategic alliances going sour. In 1998, Tenet started selling its Arizona hospitals and pulling out of joint ventures that weren't performing to expectation. Tenet gave its rights to and liabilities of Company Nurse back to Paul.

"We needed to raise more money or scale down; we did both," Paul says. "I had to change the concept."

Company Nurse's initial plan to manage individual cases for company clients took too much time and labor and was a service offered by other third-party administrators. "We were competing with companies that should have been our friends," Paul says.

He focused Company Nurse only on providing around-the-clock telephone availability of registered nurses to initially manage the injury and get it on the right track for treatment. He contracts with nurses in Colorado to answer clients' calls when a worker is injured. He contracts with data companies in Oregon and Washington to generate insurance forms.

Company Nurse has more than 1,000 clients including McDonald's, Wendy's, and Fresh Choice restaurant chains. Even though the initial joint venture didn't last, it gave Company Nurse the initial capital boost to get started.

38. VENTURE CAPITAL/ SEED CAPITAL

Few venture capital funds invest in the infancy stage
of a company, and those that do are likely to
insist on significant changes.

■ ■ ■

Hossam Salib took a layoff package in 2002 from ADC Telecommunications, where he managed a team of product developers, because he wanted to start a new company in the telecommunications industry. He started shopping his idea for Aktino Inc. of Irvine, California, to West Coast venture capitalists. At the same time he brought in three other founders—Ben Itri, Michail Tsatsanis, and Ray Nagele—with strong backgrounds in communications systems, product development, operations, and telecommunications regulatory issues—to take the idea to the next step.

Venture capital firms raise hundreds of millions of dollars from wealthy individuals, companies, and institutional investors for the purpose of buying an ownership piece of young, fast-growth companies. Venture capitalists (VCs) won't even look at most firms, and they invest in less than 1 out of every 100 deals at which they do look. It is often said that VCs don't invest in small businesses; they invest in young, big businesses. Even the best VCs have imperfect forecasting skills. In baseball parlance, they expect 1 out of 10 investments will be a home run and 3 others will be doubles. The riskiest point of investment is at the idea stage that Hossam was shopping around in 2002.

"Convincing somebody when you have nothing is very tough," says Aktino chief executive Bruce Kimble. "You have to execute or you don't get the money."

One of Hossam's pitches was to Foundation Capital in Menlo Park, California, which specializes in telecommunications, e-commerce, and Internet technologies and is willing to take a hands-on role with start-ups.

One of the key values of VCs at this early stage is their ability to introduce entrepreneurs to industry leaders and key individuals who can strengthen the management team.

Even before making any investment, Foundation Capital worked with Hossam to scale back his complex and expensive idea to one more likely to get off the ground and receive initial and follow-up investments. Aktino became a producer of a family of products that would enable telecommunications companies to deliver high-speed services to customers over existing copper-wire systems. While major telephone companies have invested heavily to convert to fiber optic lines, Aktino can serve about 1,400 smaller and rural companies that can't afford that conversion. The Foundation Capital VCs went with Hossam to talk with several potential customers about their likelihood of using Aktino's products if those items were developed. Companies are loath to make a commitment or even give statistics to start-ups, even in the company of well-respected VCs, but these conversations helped Foundation Capital assess its risk of investing in Aktino.

Foundation Capital and Aktino founders put together the terms of an $8 million seed round of investment. But the VCs had one more demand: strengthen the management team with either a new chief executive or vice president of engineering. Aktino brought in both, Bruce Kimble with 20 years of management and operating experience as the chief executive, and Willen Lao with more than 10 years of experience developing DSL technology as chief engineer.

Aktino's experience illustrates why many entrepreneurs avoid venture capital investment at the earliest stages. Demands to reshape the company, the concept, the market, and the management team are common. Entrepreneurs have to be highly flexible to secure this type of funding. Sometimes the VCs' demands are essential and correct, and sometimes they are disastrous. Aktino's flexibility secured not only Foundation Capital's support but seed investments from two other funds and a second investment round of $17 million in the fall of 2004 when the first products were delivered to customers.

39. MERGER OF PREVIOUS BUSINESS

Many serial entrepreneurs are able to start new enterprises
with the help of capital from previous companies.

■ ■ ■

Twin brothers Robert and Ryan Weber of Waite Park, Minnesota, aren't born entrepreneurs, but they're close. When they were 15, they started selling baseball collectables from an Internet site. That experience led to other online ventures, such as a banner advertising exchange and a Web portal that gave away free products in order to build valuable marketing databases. The earnings they retained from the free-products experiment helped start their current company, Freeze.com and its major subsidiary, FreeStuff-Center.com. "Our first ideas were successful enough that we made enough money that we could build on," Rob says.

Some people have business ideas they never act upon. Some try entrepreneurship once, either fail or hate it, and never go back. Some start or buy one business and stick with it for life. But others try, try again, building experience and capital for the next venture. The Webers fall into that fourth category.

"When we started in 1995 there weren't a lot of entrenched players on the Internet, so although we didn't have the capital that others did, we could still be players," Rob says. "You can take more risks when you're young."

By the time the Webers, including mom, Debby Childers, and older brother Aaron, started FreeStuffCenter.com, they had several hundred thousand dollars from previous ventures and were able to attract professional investors who wanted a piece of the Internet phenomenon. The Webers wisely put these business pros on the company board of advisors. The concept was to become the best site for quality freebies, such as screen savers and other computer desktop content. FreeStuffCenter.com's revenues were ten times greater than costs, which helped propel Rob and Ryan to the Minnesota Collegiate Entrepreneur Award from St. Cloud State University in 2000 and to runners-up for the North American Collegiate Entrepreneur Award that same year.

"We learned mostly by trial and error," Rob says. "One of the best things I learned in college entrepreneur classes was to raise money and not spend it all."

That principle proved valuable in 2001 when the technology industry struggled and venture investments were scarce after the dot-com crash, he adds. The twins also decided at that time to expand and reposition their company, renaming it Freeze.com.

"We wanted a shorter domain name. FreeStuffCenter, which became a subsidiary, didn't own its own content. And we sold some of the domain names we owned, but hadn't made profitable," Rob says. "That last thing is pretty common in our industry, but many would be shocked at the prices."

Freeze.com distributes marketing offers to online customers who have agreed to receive it by opting in to various offers. Clients pay to have their materials sent on a cost-per-lead basis. Freeze.com has more than 30 million proven responders in its database, and 15 million visitors each month, a skill learned in that first Web site and honed with every business since then. "We now have a very sophisticated survey lead generation system," Rob explains. "Only four or five companies are as sophisticated as we are."

Freeze.com has 32 employees and is growing rapidly. Its revenues in 2003 were $12 million.

SECTION E

PURSUE OTHER POSSIBILITIES
■ ■ ■

Entrepreneurs are nothing if not creative. They find resources that others might not be willing to tap. They might have to relinquish some of their favorite possessions, even a previous business, in order to raise the capital to start another venture. Typically, these new businesses have good growth prospects that make such investments worthwhile. If such resources aren't available, the entrepreneur may search for or stumble across an unusual capital source, such as a contest.

40. SPIN-OFFS

A parent company can be a source of capital and other
support when it spins off a division into a separate company.

■ ■ ■

Kott Koatings Inc. in Foothill Ranch, California, has been refinishing porcelain and fiberglass bathtubs and sinks since 1953 and franchising the concept since 1973. The company sells franchises with exclusive geographic territories and is the supplier of patented refinishing materials developed by John T. Kott.

By the mid-1990s, company revenues and franchise sales had leveled off. So son John M. Kott started looking for ways to grow the company. Because the company specializes in coatings, it developed an industrial polymer that could be sprayed on a truck bed and dry in seconds. John's brother Ken built a special machine to apply the liquid.

John M. decided to sell or lease the machines as a business opportunity with ongoing revenue from sales of the coating materials. But instead of keeping this process as a division of Kott Koatings, John spun off Vortex Sprayliners Inc. as a separate company in 2000. The Kotts own both corporations.

"Kott Koatings loaned Vortex $400,000 to develop the system," John explains. "If Vortex was just a division and was a bust, the loan couldn't have been written off. As a separate corporation, carefully split and documented, then Kott could have written off an unpaid loan."

Fortunately for the Kotts, Vortex Sprayliners took off. In four years it had more than 700 dealers compared to 230 Kott Koatings franchisees after 30 years. Vortex was quickly able to pay back the initial loan to Kott Koatings.

However, the relationship between the parent company and the spinoff provided the needed start-up capital and much more, John says. Vortex could use Kott's existing building and telephones. Kott's sales personnel also sold Vortex systems. Having that infrastructure in place is invaluable for a new company. John didn't have to divert his attention from growing Vortex in order to train a new sales staff, develop marketing plans, or negotiate leases.

Even more important, John says, is the 50 years of management experience he and his father gained from Kott Koatings.

"We always talked about if we could go back to the beginning, we would reformat Kott differently, and it would have been bigger faster," John says. "We took all of that knowledge and formatted Vortex the way we should have done with Kott."

Rather than sell franchises with exclusive territories, as Kott Koatings had done, Vortex sold business opportunities with every dealer able to sell everywhere. Some of its dealers are established auto repair shops that have added spray-on truck bed liners as an additional service. Some are located within a block of each other. But increasingly, dealers are finding other uses for the durable coating. They are applying it to floors, walls, boat trailers, and wood decks. Wal-Mart superstores have sprayed Vortex coatings on the floors of their bakeries. Previously, cooking racks rolled out of 400-degree ovens, and their wheels melted the epoxy floors. They don't even dent Vortex floors, John says.

"We have the advantage of a whole lot of people looking at the product and finding new uses for it instead of following a set franchise system," John says. "But we could not have grown this fast without the financing and knowledge from Kott Koatings."

41.
ONE COMPANY
FUNDS THE NEXT

Many business owners are serial entrepreneurs who
use the proceeds from the sale of one company
to help capitalize their next venture.

■ ■ ■

John Lown is like many American business owners. They don't stay with one business their entire careers; they start and grow several companies. John started in automotive retailing running a chain of Auto Aid auto parts stores. He invented FloTool, a pour spout for consumer-friendly motor oil plastic containers. Then he raised $350,000 from private investors to start a business making the spouts and built sales to $6.5 million annually. In 1994, John paid off all FloTool debt and recapitalized the company in order to have $9 million in capital for a new venture. It would be built around another one of his inventions that had greater revenue potential than the spout to tap a much larger home products market.

"I decided I wanted to be in manufacturing rather than retailing," John says. "I was looking at different products made with plastics. I wanted something that could be a brand name instead of a niche market."

He selected for commercialization his patented airtight seal for dry food storage containers. His market research found plenty of containers for leftover food, but few that would keep foods like crackers and cereal fresh and ant-free in home cupboards. John invested his profits from FloTool, kept some of the investors from that venture and brought in some new ones to launch Snapware Corp. in Fullerton, California.

The decision to let go of one company in order to have the capital to start another is strictly business, John says. An inventor or business owner cannot become so attached to a product or venture that he is unable to recognize strategic opportunities and make decisions in the best interest of his investors.

"I would never have been able to grow FloTool the way I could Snapware," John says. "I was looking at the future of what Snapware could be: a wonderful brand."

John developed clear plastic round jars and square containers with built-in grips. He patented the lid that can be opened or closed with a snap using one finger. He showed Snapware to customers, who suggested extensions to the basic line, such as labeling the 32-ounce square container for ground coffee and decorating the 120-ounce round jar with paw prints to be a dog biscuit holder.

Discount chains Target and Costco, specialty retailer Container Store, and pet retailers PETCO and PETsMART started stocking various versions of Snapware. Greeting card retailer Hallmark asked Snapware to make jars decorated for various seasons: ghosts for Halloween and Santas for Christmas.

Some serial entrepreneurs recognize their limitations or preferences. They have the gift for starting businesses but either cannot or do not want to run a large corporation. Some prefer to remain with the companies they started in a supporting role. Others like to move on and start something new.

Snapware is growing rapidly, not only by attracting more retail companies as customers but by adding more products. Instead of staying with dry food, Snapware has expanded to all sorts of storage products for camping, Christmas ornaments, and crafts.

"Snapware is doing well using internally generated profits to grow," John says, "but as CEO, I have to craft an exit strategy for my investors. If you bring in private equity groups representing pension funds or other large investors, there are more restrictions. They may bring in a chief executive with experience running $100 million companies. That's something an entrepreneur has to weigh when looking for expansion capital."

42. INSURANCE SETTLEMENT

A payment from an insurance company may
provide needed capital for a start-up venture.

■ ■ ■

After working two years for the State of Victoria in Australia, Amy Frey returned to the United States and worked for the dean of the graduate school of management at Georgetown University. Her job was finding internships for MBA students, and she was miserable. One rainy November day, another vehicle hit and virtually totaled her only possession, her Dodge Daytona. Amy wasn't hurt.

"It was one of the worst days I ever had," Amy says. "I felt very low. What am I doing here? How will finding internships for MBA students further my career? And then the accident."

When the $3,000 settlement check arrived from the other driver's insurance company, Amy did not repair her truck or apply the money to buying another vehicle. Instead, she used the cash to start a business of her own: ATC International Inc. in Silver Spring, Maryland.

Many people who strongly desire to start a business will redirect money from other seeming necessities to launch their plans. Amy says she didn't really think about whether she would need a car later. The check seemed to be a timely answer to her unhappiness with her career direction and impatience to move in the direction of self-employment.

First, she bought a round-trip ticket to Australia where she networked with acquaintances and won several consulting contracts from companies in that region that were ATC's first clients. "The insurance money wasn't enough by itself, but it gave me the courage to start the business," Amy says. "Being able to get some clients let me know that I had something."

When she returned to Maryland, she spent the next six months of 1991 working on ATC part time, networking with her international contacts, developing three ongoing projects, and securing first-year backing from a silent partner. She continued her Georgetown University employment to pay the bills while she got the import consulting firm off the ground.

"I didn't quit my day job until I had enough business to justify it," Amy says. "This is something I always advise people who want to start a business."

Her initial vision for ATC was to provide consulting services to Australian companies that wanted to begin exporting to the United States. She would be a sales representative for a variety of Australian products. Quickly, the company became much more.

"Now we are a warehouse and distributor, a third-party logistics provider for Australian companies," she says. "The company is much more focused."

ATC now employs five people and has warehouse facilities in Maryland and California, where most Australian goods first arrive into the United States. Amy has added New Zealand as a target for her services and facilities.

Ironically, Amy found that her previous job working with MBA students did provide great benefit to her after she started ATC. She has hired these students many times to do research and other work for her company. The students are eager to get international work experience, and they do excellent work, she says.

And yes, Amy did eventually get her Dodge repaired, but skipped the cosmetic repairs. She wanted as much capital as possible for her growing company, so she was willing to drive around in a dinged up truck, another common sacrifice for start-up entrepreneurs.

43. SELL SOMETHING OF VALUE

The drive toward entrepreneurship is so strong that
some people sell property to raise capital.

■ ■ ■

In 1977, Alice Cunningham worked for the Department of Labor. Neither she nor anyone in her family had any experience owning or running a business. Then she met her future husband, Blair Osborn, a professor at the University of Washington, and they decided to start a business so they could work together. Wooden hot tubs were a relatively unknown product that the pair believed had great growth potential. So they started Olympic Hot Tub Co. in Seattle, Washington, to construct and install these tubs. To finance the start-up, Alice sold a triplex she owned in Berkeley, California, which was a source of ongoing income. But real estate investment wasn't the type of business Alice and Blair had in mind.

"We wanted to do something together, and we believed in the future of the product," Alice explains. "But it was a huge transition from being a specialist to being the one who sells the product and empties the trash and everything else. In a small business, you're it."

Alice doesn't regret selling the triplex to start Olympic Hot Tub Co. "We had no choice; no one would lend us money," she says. "When we went to the local bank, we met with this Norwegian lady who had started in banking when women wore white gloves to work. She couldn't imagine this business."

U.S. economic history is paved with stories like Alice's. Millions of people have been willing to exchange a safe and routine job for the uncertainty of being their own boss. And they fund the transition by selling possessions of value. It is a mind-set that nonentrepreneurial people don't understand. Entrepreneurs don't make the exchange because business ownership is easier or more profitable than a job. Sometimes, the move is hard and costly, although it's usually not as risky as nonentrepreneurs imagine because fledgling business owners typically research and plan before moving. They believe in themselves and their ideas.

"You have to be so dedicated to own a business, but for me, failure was not an option," Alice says. "The hot tub potential seemed straight up, and the market wasn't saturated. Still, we had to educate customers because no one knew what hot tubs were in 1977."

Business ownership continues to be a struggle even after the company is established, she adds. At one point, she sold her collection of hundred-year-old Oriental rugs for capital to keep Olympic Hot Tub Co. going. Again, sacrifice is normal for entrepreneurs for whom failure is not an option.

"We would not still be in business if a fellow hadn't visited our store in 1982 to try to sell us portable spas that you just plug in," Alice says. "Prior to that, we were really in construction doing one tub every few days. We could install four portable spas a day, which really moved us into retailing."

Still, Alice hardly considers herself visionary. "We were really quite cautious about going all out in business," she says. "If we had bigger vision, who knows where we'd be today."

As it is, Olympic Hot Tub Co. has 40 employees, $10 million in annual sales and more than 12,000 customers in Washington and Alaska, almost half of whom have come to the company by referral of previous customers. Olympic Hot Tub Co. has four stores, and it has repeatedly made the annual list of largest companies in the pool and spa industry compiled by trade journal *AQUA* magazine.

44. EBAY SALES

Determined entrepreneurs can raise capital to help
finance a fledgling business by selling excess
merchandise on Internet auctions.

■ ■ ■

Danny Archibald had been working at auto dealerships since he was 16 when he started by washing the cars. His father, John, worked at a Honda dealer. After the corporation bought out John's employer, and replacement jobs were hard to find, father and son decided to open their own car sales business. Dealerships for the most popular car brands are difficult and costly to obtain, so in 2001 the two men started Archibald's Inc., a Kennewick, Washington, retailer of expensive, preowned vehicles including BMW, Cadillac, Lexus, and Mercedes. While they used some personal funds and a bank loan for part of the start-up costs, Danny also turned to online auction powerhouse, eBay, to raise some capital.

"I determined to sell anything I didn't have to have: power tools, guitars, art work, a Rolex watch," Danny says. "I sold anything I could buy again later. In 2001 there was less competition selling on eBay than there is now."

Tens of millions of people buy and sell on eBay, the biggest and busiest online auction site. For many, eBay selling is a full-time business. But for far more people, it is a way to raise extra cash as Danny did. Unlike a swap meet or garage sale, Danny could tap into eBay's audience of more than 50 million registered users. When there was less competition, sellers could get better prices even for common products. Today, eBay is best known as a wholesale shopper's marketplace, even though relatively rare products bring above-market prices. eBay encourages casual sellers by making it simple to list one or several items, use templates, create listings with eBay's design editor, track selling activities, and print shipping labels and invoices.

The process was simple and more lucrative than any other means of selling possessions to help launch Archibald's Inc., Danny says. "Today, I could go buy it all back if I wanted. It's not like I sold my home and moved into a ratty apartment."

The capital he made on eBay helped get Archibald's off the ground. Its 2003 sales were $9.6 million and growing fast. The Archibalds buy their cars from manufacturers and dealers to whom drivers return the vehicles when their leases expire. The Archibalds have known the manufacturers from their years working in the industry.

"We work hard to give our name a good reputation in this area," Danny says. "We built a new building in a nice part of town. Selling high-end used cars gives us credibility in the market."

Archibald's has two full-time salespeople and two other employees in addition to Danny and John.

Business ownership wasn't Danny's burning dream. "I liked working for other people. Dealers paid me a lot for how young I was," he says. "But those jobs don't last a long time. Today, it doesn't feel like we're owners.

We're working hard all the time. It sometimes feels like we're office managers."

Even so, he shrugs off his eBay sales days as merely a means to get into business, a capital-raising activity that any entrepreneur would use if necessary. "It wasn't really a sacrifice," Danny says. "I had way too much stuff."

45. WIN A BUSINESS PLAN COMPETITION

A well-written business plan might be a winner even
before you submit it to investors or lenders.

■ ■ ■

Many commercial and residential building and remodeling projects in Connecticut threw away tons of usable, salvageable material. Some of it was being shipped as far away as Ohio because New England landfills were running out of space. John Powers and some friends in West Hartford, Connecticut, wanted to salvage those materials in order to save landfills and provide low-cost building materials for home revitalization. Their concept was to open a store like the Salvation Army Thrift Store to sell used lumber, shingles, pipes, and other building products. They incorporated The ReCONNstruction Center as a nonprofit entity.

Funding was a challenge until one of the center's advisory board members spotted on an Internet listserv an announcement of Ford Motor Co.'s BEST (Building Entrepreneurial Success Today) Business Plan competition in 2004. Grand prize was $50,000, and there were two $25,000 prizes for runners-up.

"None of us had experience writing a business plan," says John, president of the center's board of directors. "We had already worked a year-and-a-half on the plan. We did a lot of research on similar stores. I visited four of them several times. We got hold of three other business plans from similar operations. We changed their formulas based on what we wanted to say."

Ford sponsored the business plan competition as part of its longstanding commitment to entrepreneurship and support for communities in which it does business. The auto company is not alone in such endeavors. Many universities across the country sponsor business plan competitions. Many of those contests emphasize technology or appeal to venture capitalists. Ford's criteria included overall benefit to the community, viability of success, funding requirements, anticipated sales, analysis of competition, and overall presentation.

Ford asked members of SCORE, a nationwide volunteer business counseling organization sponsored by the U.S. Small Business Administration, to judge the several thousand entries. The winner would also be assigned to a SCORE counselor for further help in developing the business.

John believes The ReCONNstruction Center's plan had an advantage of 18 months of preparation instead of just the contest's three-month duration.

"We were really proud of our plan," John says. "One component that was very important that I think we fulfilled well was benefit to the community. We're helping revitalize the housing stock. We have [in Connecticut] a lot of turn-of-the-century housing that needs help to fix up. We want to get people to have a stake in their homes by having access to affordable building products."

In order to meet the 20-page limit that the Ford contest imposed, The ReCONNstruction Center had to reduce the type size from 12 points to 10 points on the plan it submitted.

The center won first place and used the $50,000 prize money to help launch the first store in New Britain, Connecticut. Builders in the area now have a place to donate and get a tax deduction for usable materials they have torn out during remodeling projects.

The winning business plan has a value beyond Ford's prize money. It has helped John and his board make The ReCONNstruction Center a reality and given other potential financial backers greater confidence in the viability of the project.

"I'm the type of person who needs to write things down; it helps me think," John says. "Most grant institutions want something in writing during the application process too, maybe not a typical business plan but they may want to know you have one. Now we do."

PART 3

CONSERVING CAPITAL TO STAY AHEAD OF THE MONEY SEARCH

■ ■ ■

Most of this book is about sources and methods of raising capital to start, operate, or grow a business. However, this section focuses on an important aspect of financing your own business, which is making the most of the money your venture does have. Some of it seems obvious: Don't spend every dime you make. However, the secret is discipline. An entrepreneur whose personal finances are in shambles will find this lack of discipline carries over into business. Financial problems can become worse because the owner is the last one paid, and many owners report going without any salary for a few months or even years in order to have more capital for the business.

In addition to self-discipline, the business owner can use financial tools to conserve and maximize capital. These tools, including a budget, a strategic plan, and a financial forecast, help owners better understand their company finances and goals. Many business owners delegate financial management to outside accountants or inside subordinates, which is a mistake if they abdicate decision-making responsibility as well. Owners need to know how to read their financial statements. They need to recognize when the company is struggling financially even as revenues climb. They need to know how to monitor cash flow and project costs. And they need to learn how to increase the productivity within their companies, which means getting more work out of the same or smaller workforce. Technology, of course, is one key to greater productivity, but so is management of people and time. Unless the owner understands how operations mesh with spending, he or she will have difficulty making tough choices between cutting costs and making strategic capital investments.

Financial discipline, in addition to keeping the owner aware of the status of the company's capital, may reward the company with lower costs of borrowing and waiver of some standard expenses.

46.

LIVE BENEATH
YOUR MEANS

Successful business owners cultivate the personal and
professional habit of not spending every dime they make.

■ ■ ■

John Jordan has worked for both large and small marketing and communications agencies in San Francisco and Washington, D.C. In 2002, he
decided it was time to start his own public relations company, Principor
Communications in Washington, D.C. John's lifetime habit of spending
less than he makes has been the single best capital preservation strategy he
has adopted.

"My wife and I have always lived below our means," John says. "Con-
sumption has just never been high on our priority list."

Most successful entrepreneurs adopt the same strategy. It is a discipline that is easier for some business owners than others. For people like
John, it is second nature. He can't remember a time in his personal or professional life that he struggled to keep spending below 100 percent of revenues. For others, this is a difficult habit to cultivate, especially in modern
society with easy access to credit and the constant bombardment of information about all the goodies that make life or business easier or more fun.
You don't just need a computer. You need a faster one with more memory
and larger monitor. You don't just need a cup of coffee. You need a triple
latte decaffeinated at $4 a mug.

John's perspective on money isn't so much one of calculated saving on
a regular basis as it is contentment with not spending money even when the
business bank account has enough to cover nine months of regular expenses. Clients highly regard this discipline, even if they are not directly
aware of it. John specializes in public relations for smaller and start-up
companies, primarily in technology.

"I have managed my share of clients who wanted to spend money like
crazy," John says. "But especially after the technology bust, most are very
cost-conscious. Mid- and small-sized companies that used to go with the
brand-name public relations company now realize that [approach] may not
necessarily give them the best value."

The clients ultimately pay for the highrise suites and fancy furnishings of their service providers and professional advisors. More of these clients are looking for better value instead of opulent ambiance.

"I keep a very low overhead; that is definitely a deliberate thing," John says. "If I have a number of options when buying something, I look for best value which is not necessarily the most expensive.

"Part of my approach in public relations is that the client is buying my talent and the talent of my staff," John adds. "I want that to be clear to the client. If they are looking for a lot of atmosphere, that's not what I want to offer."

Principor works as a strategic partner, not just a hired gun, with companies across the nation. John's financial discipline communicates that Principor is as careful with clients' money as it is with its own.

Yet John doesn't feel deprived because of this discipline. "There are certain things I'd like to have for the business, but I distinguish between needs and wants," he says. "In a lot of public relations agencies, they hire more people before they actually get business. Then they lay people off. I don't want to get into a pattern like that. I would rather build infrastructure and hire a little behind the work. That allows my employees to stretch in the sense of having opportunities to try different things they might not in a larger agency."

47. NO PAYCHECK

People who start new businesses should plan their personal finances to enable them to go without a regular salary for as long as a year to preserve capital for the fledgling enterprise.

■ ■ ■

After building and selling a technology company, John Lee Shetrone Jr. took time off to honor the noncompete clause in his sale contract. Then he started Vision Technologies Inc. in Glen Burnie, Maryland, in 2000 with three partners. John put up the initial $320,000 from the sale of his previous company but retains only 61 percent ownership of the new venture, Vision Technologies. The other partners own varying percentages of the professional information technology services and network integration firm. Everyone has an equal vote and they all make the same salary. In addition, John set aside 10 percent for valued stakeholders who were willing to join the company for less salary because they believed in the upside potential when it eventually is sold.

"We're not shy about saying that we are building Vision Technologies to sell," John says. "It's a moral thing to let these employees benefit from working here."

But each partner "bought" his way into Vision Technologies with a commitment to go without a salary for six months. And then they agreed to take below-market wages after that. John's $60,000 salary was 20 percent of his salary at his previous company.

Most owners of new businesses must forego wages in the initial months or even years. The longer they can restrain from taking capital out of the company, the stronger it can be. The practice serves many purposes, John says.

"We wanted to minimize cash outlay to make sure the company had the kind of performance so that the banks would see profits as soon as possible and as large as possible," he explains.

"The second reason is commitment. You wake up with a different attitude when the only way to get compensated is for the company to succeed," John says. "It's buy-in. You have to put skin in the game. You have to contribute sweat equity."

"Third, when you hire new employees and tell them you are not taking a salary, they see owner commitment that they don't see at a gazillion-dollar company," he says.

The owners must lead by example and set the tone that the company will be frugal with its capital. If employees agree to come in at a lower salary, they are sure the owner isn't making a financial killing on their sacrifice. The owners' salary waiver also sends a message to bankers that these partners won't raid the company and leave an indebted shell.

"The banks bought into us more because of our action," John says, adding that banks have given Vision Technologies four lines of credit that give the company the financial strength to sign multimillion-dollar contracts. The company has no long-term debt.

"If we want to get beyond personal guarantees for lines of credit, we must prove sustainable growth," John adds.

That growth has been exceptionally strong. Starting with two employees in 2000, it has 109 employees now. In 2003, Vision Technologies was the fastest growing privately owned company and 13th-largest network integrator in the Baltimore, Maryland, region. Its clients include Hewlett-Packard, Discovery Channel, and the Federal Deposit Insurance Corporation.

But the no-salary rule still applies. When a new manager joined the company in 2004, he had to go six months without pay. "That's the cost of sitting at the table," John explains.

48. LIVE ON A BUDGET

A company cannot maximize its capital merely by
growing revenue. It must also control spending.

■ ■ ■

As a student at the Minneapolis College of Art and Design, David Fowlkes invented an automobile wheel that continues to spin after the tire stops. It was eight years before David, Ian Hardman, and Hank Seemore started Davin Wheel Co. in Providence, Rhode Island, in 1998 to sell the patented wheels. Even though the custom, luxury wheels attracted such wealthy customers as National Basketball Association center Shaquille O'Neal and National Football League stars Donovan McNabb and Jerry Rice, Davin Wheel started with one employee and less than $5,000.

"For a small company like Davin Wheel, it is absolutely vital to live within a budget," says Ian, who is the company's chief executive. "We set out our annual budget in October or November for the following year, but our budgeting process takes place every week. We're constantly looking at how revenues are trending, not just how this month compares to last year."

Davin Wheel makes 75 percent of its revenues in the first six months of the year. The first warm day following the snow and cold of winter, car enthusiasts rush out and wash their vehicles and want to buy a product that will make them stand out. Continuous motion wheels certainly do that. Still, wheels that cost several thousand dollars each are a dispensable luxury in a weak economy, so Davin Wheel must watch the direction of sales each month and not wait until the end of the year to make adjustments.

"If sales are not trending up, we are proactive to ask what spending we can manage," Ian says. "We try to be very thoughtful about it, not have a knee-jerk reaction."

For example, one of the budget areas to adjust is marketing, but simply cutting back might not be the right solution. Florida is a good custom wheel market, but after four hurricanes hit Florida in 2004, residents were busy cleaning up and not thinking about buying car products. As Davin Wheel rolled out some new products, it postponed its marketing campaign in Miami and reallocated resources to California, another big car market where the company has a manufacturing plant.

If a product line doesn't sell as well as expected, Davin Wheel must adjust quickly and maybe even drop the line completely, Ian says. Major public companies with greater resources would be slower to take necessary corrective action.

While gross revenues may sound impressive, the important number to watch in order to live within a budget, Ian says, is earnings before interest, taxes, depreciation, and amortization are subtracted, which accountants call EBITDA. "It's a moving target. We adjust every month based on that number, and the only two ways to do that are either to grow revenues or manage expenses."

The continuous watch on the budget has helped Davin Wheel grow from a 1,000-square-foot plant in California in 2002 to 12,000 square feet after three months to 70,000 square feet in 2005.

"Fast growth is a high-quality problem to have," Ian says, "but sustainable growth is more important. Growing revenues implies growing costs too. If growth gets out of hand, you can lose control of the whole company. We set our sights to grow 30 percent a year, not 1,000 percent. And watching our budget closely is part of doing that."

49. STRATEGIC PLANNING

A framework for making decisions about which contracts
to pursue and capabilities to exploit enables a
company to maximize its capital.

■ ■ ■

Lisa Williams is a self-described planner at heart. The engineer wants to know every detail of a bid or project and its impact on her company, 3D Research Corp. in Huntsville, Alabama, before one step is taken. That's why she's a big believer in strategic planning, to which she attributes 3D Research's growth from one woman in 1997 to more than 150 employees.

Strategic planning helps even the most efficient, streamlined companies wring the most profit out of their capabilities by clearly defining their capabilities, creative position, and future markets. Most companies don't have a strategic plan because they confuse it with other well-known business tools. A strategic plan is shorter and less detailed than a business plan, although the former can provide the foundation and framework for the latter. A strategic plan is more visionary and longer term than an operational plan. Still, a strategic plan is not pie in the sky. It focuses on what is realistic and attainable for the company.

"Our strategic plan is not a limit as much on the number of projects we go after as on the things we have the highest chance of winning," Lisa explains. "If we go after 20 contracts and only have a reasonable chance of winning five, then we waste a lot of money on those other 15. We want to put our resources into the thing we have a high probability of winning."

3D Research is a government contractor with capabilities in systems engineering, meteorological support services, testing, and evaluation. Government payments tend to lag 60 to 90 days, so 3D Research must have the capital to survive in the interim, Lisa says. Furthermore, 3D Research must have the ability to add staff and equipment for contracts it wins before receiving payment. A recent winning bid required the company to hire 20 people adding $100,000 to its monthly payroll. That kind of growth takes strategic planning.

"Before we go after a project, we ask how much do we have, how much do we need if we get it, how much in bonuses can we pay out," Lisa says. "If we have to put money up front for equipment, we'd better be sure we have that money."

This type of planning helps a company establish a benchmark and monitor performance as a contract proceeds, and that experience becomes a building block for the next strategic plan and project.

Even though strategic planning comes naturally to Lisa, it is not easy. 3D Research brings in a disinterested third party to run the strategic planning sessions because Lisa is concerned that employees would tend to try to do what they think she wants instead of thinking strategically about what is best for the company's long-term growth. These strategy sessions help clarify how to build on strengths, resolve weaknesses, exploit opportunities, and avoid threats, putting the so-called SWOT analysis into shaping a company's future.

"We've always been financially strong and never had to borrow, although we do have lines of credit," Lisa says. "The reason we're able to do that is because of strategic planning."

50. STRONG BANKING RELATIONSHIPS

Companies that need capital must develop and maintain
good relationships with bankers who understand their
business and will fight for their funding needs.

■ ■ ■

After working at the family Christmas wreath and tree farm, John and Chris Mickman decided to start Mickman Brothers Landscaping in Minnesota in 1975. They started on a shoestring and a year later bought their father's part-time Christmas wreath manufacturing company, which sold 15,000 wreaths in Minneapolis and St. Paul, Minnesota. In 1979, Mickman Brothers had a cash shortfall because a landscaping job with the state highway department didn't go as planned. John decided to seek a loan from a banker who had financed the landscaping firm's first pickup truck. John had all his personal and business accounts at that small community bank.

"Before I went to talk to this banker, I wrote a plan for how to get out of the problem," John says. "I was just a young kid. I was so nervous."

As he waited for his appointment, John overheard the banker scolding another business owner and turning down a request for more money. The longer John listened, the worse he felt. Nevertheless, when his turn came, he explained the history of Mickman Brothers Landscaping and the recovery plan.

"He had a number of questions and then he said, 'OK. This is a good plan. I'm certain I can swing this with the loan committee,' and he did," John says.

That's when John learned the value of a good banker who works to understand your business and will fight for the capital that business needs to survive and grow. Still, John had done his part by developing a detailed, written plan to prove that Mickman Brothers was a viable business and that John and Chris were worth an investment of time and money. Mickman Brothers stayed with that officer as he moved from bank to bank as such people often do. During that time, the company started shipping Christmas wreaths outside Minnesota and opened a garden center and golf driving range in Ham Lake to add to their landscaping and irrigation work.

The company's business is highly seasonal, partly because it is located in Ham Lake, Minnesota, whose winters are long, and partly because half the revenue comes from Christmas wreaths. To make the cash flow situation even tougher, many of the 600,000 wreaths the company makes annually are sold through fundraising events with schools and nonprofit clubs. Mickman Brothers finances that $5 million in business until it is repaid from the fundraising revenues in December.

John's favorite bank officer finally moved to Florida, and Mickman Brothers stayed with that officer's last employer, one of the largest banks.

"In the course of the next two years, I kid you not, I had four different bankers," John says. "When the fourth one left, the lending manager called me and wanted to bring over a new guy. I told him I was tired of banking with these guys, teaching them about my business so they could go to bat for me with the loan committee and then they leave. I called up another banker I knew before at a smaller community bank and switched. He wanted to meet me, know about my business so he could match me with the right person on his staff."

John stresses the importance of a business owner shopping around for the right banking relationship. By getting to know several bank officers, the owner can find one with whom he is comfortable as well as a bank that has the resources and services that the owner's business needs. No single bank can fit every company's need. If the relationship changes and the bank no longer meets the company's needs, don't be afraid to switch to a banking relationship that works for you, John advises.

"My business is fun for me. One of the things I enjoy is the relationship with the bank if I have someone I enjoy," John says. "In my experience, if you don't have a good relationship with a banker, it is so taxing on you. In good years and bad, I was always able to get the money I needed for growth."

51. ESTABLISH CREDIT EARLY

From the beginning, make it clear to vendors that your company pays promptly in order to earn credit terms for large projects.

■ ■ ■

When Tim Williams and Craig Woerz launched Media Storm, a media planning and buying agency in Norwalk, Connecticut, in 2001, they wrote into the pro forma financial statement of their business plan the need to prepay their initial purchases of time and space in major media.

"I had been in the cable industry since 1980, my partner since 1990, so we recognized that we may have to prepay invoices because media don't extend credit to start-ups," Tim explains. "That was part of our initial capitalization."

Sure enough, their very first project in November 2001 was to buy 30-second commercial time on a national cable network to promote a movie.

Media Storm doesn't create ads; it strategizes with clients to determine the most effective placement of their advertisements and then buys time on cable or network television or space in print media. The media buys are billed to clients, who may not pay right away.

Tim and Craig had the $50,000 on hand to prepay that first invoice. Their early action gave them a quick-pay track record to point to as they started buying advertising space and commercial time for other clients. Only sporadically did other media require prepayment, Tim says.

"A few months later, we came back to that cable network, and they granted us credit because we had a track record of paying them," he says.

Once that good credit is established, Tim adds, it is imperative to manage cash flow so that the company pays bills on time even when vendors extend credit.

"Once we started, we were dealing with million-dollar projects," he says. "We certainly didn't want to pay those amounts up front or borrow money to pay our bills. We got a line of credit, but we have never had to use it. The advertising world works on fixed [profit] margins. We don't want to pay interest on loans, which decreases our profits."

Media Storm now has a client list that includes FX, Showtime, Tribune Entertainment, WE Network, and Gold's Gym. Media Storm buys tens of millions of dollars in advertising time and space from 700 media vendors. It could not survive if it had to prepay those invoices. But by establishing credit early and managing payments all along, Media Storm can pay later.

"Very quickly we started buying a lot of media around the country," Tim says. "Being able to point back to good media credit references established our reputation with major cable and newspaper companies. Yes, they do check references. It's not enough to say that you pay."

Tim acknowledges that his and Craig's reputations in the cable industry helped them win clients and vendors.

"Have a good plan that lets you operate in an industry in which you have intimate knowledge," he advises. "If we tried to add the health sector, we might have the greatest media strategy in the world but we would have no reputation or contacts. Those allow you in the door."

Media Storm has grown rapidly to 15 employees, but the growth has been strategic and managed. "It's important to have a core competency," Tim says. "Ours is the entertainment industry. We have turned down business that's not a fit or would cause us to grow too fast."

52. FINANCIAL FORECASTING

If you can accurately forecast business income and expenses,
you can plan for the least costly source of capital or avoid
spending that depletes cash at the wrong time.

■ ■ ■

Brian and Jennifer England had a personal habit of living within
their means before starting British American Auto Care Inc. in Columbia,
Maryland, in 1976. To do that, they had to know what their means were going to be. They carried that mind-set into business.

"I just presumed everyone had a budget at home," Brian says. "If you
can't handle your day-to-day expenses how are you going to do it at your
business?"

The Englands carefully listed each personal and business expense, including Brian's salary. Then they calculated how many hours of auto repair
work British American Auto Care would have to do to break even. In 1976
it was 35 hours.

"We sell hours. Labor costs so much per hour, hours become money.
[Sale of] parts are icing," Brian explains. "We started business with
$10,000, which would meet all our expenses for six months. If we had no
work, we could survive [in business] six months. Every day we had work,
that was one more day the business would survive: six months and one day,
six months and two days."

Brian was doing the simplest form of financial forecasting. Figure all
your expenses and sources of income. If they aren't at least equal, you
shouldn't even start the business. Forecasting needs to be a routine part of
managing a business in order to maximize resources. If you fail to forecast
the amount of capital needed, you may run out of cash. The choice then
may be between unplanned borrowing at a high interest rate or unfavorable
terms and panic selling of assets that brings less than top dollar. Inaccurate
forecasts may lead to borrowing that the company can't afford or excess
inventory that ties up capital and is expensive to handle and store.

Forecasting is difficult for the start-up because it is an educated guess,
based on research of similar types of businesses and assumptions about
costs and revenue. "You have to be honest with yourself about your fore-

cast numbers," Brian says. Many entrepreneurs underestimate the time and money they need to start and grow their ventures. Financial forecasting, especially in the early years of business, should include three calculations: the worst-case scenario, the everything-goes-as-planned scenario, and the beyond-your-wildest-dreams scenario. As the owner monitors actual business performance week by week or month by month, he adjusts each track. Companies are considered good financial forecasters if they are 85 percent accurate. You might think lenders and investors would be delighted if you wildly underestimate financial performance, but they prefer business owners who understand their businesses and industries so well that they hit their forecasts precisely.

Many small businesses encounter seasonal fluctuations. For a farmer or Christmas tree salesman, such fluctuations are easy to predict. But some industries are less obvious, such as midsummer slowdowns for business services or early April ebbs for seminar planners. Such trends become more predictable the longer a business is open if the owner is tracking financial data, and that knowledge will help plan for seasonal financing that best suits the company.

For British American Auto Care, the fluctuations are less tied to seasons of the year than to company growth over time, Brian says. From the initial 35 work hours to cover expenses, the company now needs 282 work hours. "Unless we expand, the number stays remarkably the same year after year. You can find complicated forecasting models and software, but it gets down to basics. I prefer to keep it simple."

53. MONITOR CASH FLOW

Profit is an accounting term. If a company is profitable on paper
but runs out of cash, it's out of business, so continually
analyzing cash flow is vital for survival.

■ ■ ■

After a proposed partnership didn't pan out, Jason Beans started consulting in Chicago, Illinois, in 1996, work that evolved in 1999 into Rising

Medical Solutions Inc. The practice helps companies manage their workers compensation, auto liability, and medical insurance claims.

"I started in a major cash hole," Jason says. "I put everything on credit cards, liquidated my 401(k), and sold my house in Boston. Watching cash became critical."

Cash businesses like restaurants have fewer problems with cash flow. But service businesses like Rising Medical Solutions can have serious cash flow crises if the owner doesn't watch payables and receivables carefully. Jason can have 30 days of expenses before he sends out his bills. Many clients take 30 days or longer to pay. He is methodical and persistent in getting payment, some of which come in as long as two years later.

When Jason first studied his profit and loss statements, he didn't distinguish between accrual profit and cash profit. The former records income when a sale is made and expenses when the goods or services are received, regardless of when the client's check arrives or when the entrepreneur pays a bill. It gives a more accurate picture of profitability, but profit doesn't pay the rent. The cash method of accounting records income when the client's check is in hand and records expenses when the entrepreneur actually pays a bill.

"When I switched to cash [accounting], I was shocked at the peaks and valleys of cash flow," Jason says. "I keep on my wall each month both my cash profit, for short-term planning, and accrual profit, for long term. It's in my face every day. I can see trends and jump on a problem right away."

Businesses need to forecast cash flow to avoid running out of money during seasonal dips or if unexpected problems arise. If cash runs out, borrowing can be an expensive drain on company growth for a long time.

"Besides, most service businesses will have a difficult time going the bank route," Jason says. "Mine is a service that is capital intensive—software and computers—but that's capital that banks will not often use as collateral."

In addition to diligence in collecting receivables and watching cash, Jason has established an emergency fund equal to at least four months of expenses. "You're not going to run a business perfectly; expenses will come up that you don't expect," he says. "You have to be able to pay bills for four months even if no money comes in."

Jason also plans for growth by negotiating contracts that will automatically give Rising Medical Solutions bigger discounts for volume purchases. "Most suppliers will give this up front because they don't think you will reach that level," Jason says. "It helps me because my prices drop as my revenues go up."

One of the most problematic issues for Rising Medical Solutions is tax planning. As income increases, so do taxes. A company pays its year-end tax bill around March 31 and its first quarter estimated taxes for the current year a few days later. Payroll taxes for 45 employees must be deposited regularly as well.

"Capital and cash flow were a constant issue for us until we were able to achieve a certain level," Jason says, "and even now, I feel the need to monitor and control the situation on an ongoing basis."

54. EFFECTIVE RECEIVABLES COLLECTION

Late-paying customers cost your company money by tying up capital in what is essentially an interest-free loan.

■ ■ ■

Since 1984, Deborah Brooks has been providing contract and temporary workers for a variety of customers, and since 1989, she has been doing it through her own company, Arose Recruiting Company, Inc. of Newport Beach, California. She specializes in information technology, financial, and building industry companies as her clients.

"I have never not been paid by any client," Deborah says.

That result is not accidental. Arose Recruiting has a careful and consistent system for collecting receivables in a timely way. The vast majority of people and companies do pay their bills on time. However, the longer a bill is unpaid, the less likely it will be paid. The Commercial Law League of America says that 74 percent of bills delinquent for three months are paid. Less than 29 percent of those a year late are ever paid. So the quicker the vendor is to peruse overdue receivables, the better.

Overdue receivables are more than a nuisance. The unpaid supplier is in reality making an interest-free loan to the customer. Also the supplier's cash flow is hurt so it may have to sell or borrow against its receivables, which costs money. Capital tied up in unpaid receivables is a missed opportunity to invest that money in personnel, equipment, or facilities. A company can't have capital invested in an asset that earns nothing. Even modest improvements in accounts receivable collection can be big money. If a company with $3.4 million in receivables can cut the average payment lag from 50 days to 35 days, it reaps $1 million in improved cash flow.

Deborah is very careful about whom she accepts as clients. When potential clients contact Arose Recruiting or one of the salespeople brings in new clients, they are checked out with Dun & Bradstreet and banking references.

These new clients know that Deborah expects to be paid promptly. A clear credit policy is the foundation for good customer relations and timely payments. Clients are more willing to accept a policy consistently and equally applied than if you let them slide and then change tactics later. You should charge interest on the overdue amount. However, past laxness does not doom your company to late-paying customers forever. Begin at once to adhere to your credit terms with new customers and to work diligently to bring existing customers into compliance. Call them immediately when a bill is due and remind them of the terms while reaffirming how important they are to your company.

"I had a client that was an agency like Arose Recruiting, and when it was late paying, I called," Deborah says. "Their clients hadn't paid them. I said, 'I don't do business with companies that don't pay their bills. I cut you off.' I'm real harsh about that. It's hard to stay in business if you don't get paid."

Some companies encourage swift payment by offering discounts for invoices paid early. A common offer is 2 percent discount if paid within ten days of the invoice date. Occasionally, a customer will pay the discounted price after 30 days. It's vital not to allow that liberty. Discounts must be earned.

Require delinquent customers to pay cash on delivery of more products or services plus a percentage of the past-due amount until the account is current. If the customer won't commit to an acceptable payment plan or make subsequent payments on time, turn them over to an outside collections firm.

"You cannot survive in business if you don't have good receivable collections," Deborah says. "A lot of business owners hate to turn clients away, but you have to be conservative about whom you do business with."

55. MAXIMIZE PRODUCTIVITY

Doing more work in the same length of time or using lower-
priced materials are productivity improvements that can
boost a company's financial situation.

■ ■ ■

Jim Winterle was a well-respected broker of mail services for major package delivery companies, when some of his big customers asked why he didn't start a company to consolidate the international mail from many companies in order to get high-volume shipping discounts. He agreed if these customers would support him with their international mail business. Jim opened International Delivery Solutions (IDS) LLC in Milwaukee, Wisconsin, in 1999.

With just six employees in the beginning, IDS couldn't waste time or personnel. Efficiency was—and is—the key to profitability and success. So Jim has a program to maximize productivity that has enabled IDS to handle with just 40 employees 400,000 pounds of mail each month to Canada and 125,000 pounds to other countries.

Productivity improvement is a popular concept in companies of all sizes. Productivity improvements include eliminating redundancy and inefficiencies, doing work faster, buying lower-cost materials, and keeping the workforce as lean as possible. During the 1990s, new technology—fax machines, computers, cell phones, copiers that collate and staple documents automatically, and the Internet—enabled huge productivity gains in companies that made the right investments. At the same time, the amazing reduction in price of so much of the technology further boosted profitability. However, companies need to be careful not to sacrifice quality in pursuit of lower prices, or declining sales will neutralize any productivity gains.

But maximizing productivity doesn't happen by chance, Jim says. At IDS, maximizing productivity depends on hiring experienced workers and constantly training them, setting goals, keeping good records, centralizing processes, and becoming ever more automated.

Experienced workers are more efficient than novices. From the start, Jim had key people in mind to hire as soon as the company could afford them.

"We also set work goals and incentivize people with money," Jim says. "If they hit efficiency goals, they receive a bonus. The bonus for shop workers is based on how much mail they can process measured by number of pieces and weight. Management staff bonuses are based on profitability."

Everyone in the company must work together to achieve the greatest efficiencies, Jim adds. The shop workers have to have mail to work with. If the sales staff doesn't bring in enough mail, the entire process is inefficient.

IDS must keep good records in order to identify bottlenecks in the production process and sales personnel who aren't meeting their goals. The company bought ACT! contact management software to improve the sellers' efficiency and bought MAS 90 accounting software to improve financial tracking throughout the operation.

To centralize the mail processing for maximum efficiency, IDS has distribution centers in St. Louis, Kansas City, Milwaukee, and Niagara Falls, Ontario. "Also, the more automated we can get with machinery, the more productive we are," Jim says. "The mail consolidation industry started with hand work and now most of it is done by machine. I don't want to lose good employees by automation, so we grow the business to keep the employees we have busy, but we don't have to hire new ones."

56.   KEEP AN EYE
ON JOB COSTS

Unexpected or unplanned expenses can drain
much-needed capital from even experienced companies.

■ ■ ■

Darrell Stolhand is in an industry where he must sell his products and services before he knows all of his exact costs. Yet the owner of Stolhand Heating & Air Conditioning in Ponca City, Oklahoma, has thrived since 1977 because he systematically monitors every cost on every commercial and residential job.

Every business owner should control expenses and evaluate the status of expenses frequently. Such practices strengthen a company's balance sheet, reduce the need to borrow or to use lines of credit frequently, and free up cash for other purposes, such as taking advantage of discounts or sales. Back in the high-inflationary 1970s in which Darrell's father Fred started the heating and air-conditioning installation and servicing business, cost monitoring was often frustrating because it was impossible to know at any given time what supplies would cost even a few weeks later. In the early 2000s, inflation has been so low that busy owners may be tempted to skip the close supervision of expenditures. Numerous software packages are now available to track current costs and past practices, which can be built into future pricing bids. That automated recordkeeping can be important for companies like Stolhand Heating & Air Conditioning, which has added equipment such as air purifiers and services such as duct cleaning over the years. It also standardizes the pricing activity as the staff has grown to 22 employees.

Some job costs are more predictable than others, such as the number of hours an installation will take, Darrell says. By keeping records from previous years, he can estimate fairly accurately the hours and tools needed for routine jobs. Even so, he has to judge the setting and circumstances for the equipment installation that might make the job more difficult or require more time.

However, supplies can present a different challenge. "It can become pretty dangerous because you get lax," Darrell says. "Then you have a rapid increase that you didn't expect, and it impacts your profitability on each project. Not too long ago we saw a 40 percent increase in flat-steel prices in six months. You can't price a job right if you don't know your costs."

Darrell is constantly in touch with his suppliers and watches economic and industry news trying to foresee any price changes. When he gives a price on a prospective job he usually sets a time limit and advises that after 15 days, adjustments may be required.

"Owners of big commercial jobs want to lock in prices, so they don't like those deadlines; residential customers are more understanding," he says. That distinction is significant because as much as 70 percent of his work is with commercial customers. "What I try to do on commercial jobs is shorten my lead times as much as possible. I wait until the last minute to get a quote from my suppliers and submit my price to the customer at the last possible time. If I don't, not only might prices changes but I'm tying up funds earlier in the process so it's not available for my other cash needs."

Once a job begins, Darrell carefully oversees progress and expenses to avoid cost overruns. That information is important not only for the current job, but helps establish the company's track record that influences pricing on future jobs.

57.

NEGOTIATE
PAYMENT TERMS

Work hard to get favorable contract terms that will protect
business cash flow as much as possible.

Every contract is a potential cash flow killer at Cougar Turbine Supply LP in Conroe, Texas. The company buys, refurbishes, and resells used Solar turbines and engines at prices ranging from $300,000 to $1 million or more. One overhaul can take four months. If the turbine seller won't accept extended terms for the purchase price, then Cougar must get part of or the entire resale price up front from the buyer, says President Allen Shearer. "It's devastating to our cash flow to have a piece of equipment at those prices sitting in our shop for four months."

Allen and his two partners must carefully negotiate every contract to buy an engine or turbine or to find, overhaul, and sell a specific piece of equipment for Cougar Turbine Supply to make the most of its capital and avoid costly borrowing.

Cougar's customers are oil and natural gas companies around the world. Only a handful of competitors have the financial resources and the technical expertise to buy and overhaul the expensive machinery that Cougar's customers need.

"If we have extra cash, we might buy surplus equipment without having an immediate buyer for it because we can get equipment much cheaper if it's not needed," Allen says. "A turbine might cost me $75,000. But as soon as the seller knows I have a contract and need the equipment right away, the price might be $300,000. I get much better terms if they need to sell rather than I need to buy."

More often, Allen does not buy equipment until he receives an order from an oil or gas company. When Allen gets an order for a specific turbine or engine, he builds into the delivery date the time it will take to overhaul the equipment and perhaps a little time to find the machine, "but the customer needs it so it won't wait forever for delivery," he says. Allen negotiates with the customer to pay as much of the contract up front as possible, which is sometimes delicate because the customer is trying to preserve as much of its cash as possible as well.

"It's tough being a small company with limited capital in this industry," he says of Cougar, which has 15 employees and 2003 sales in excess of $9 million. "Our competitors are General Electric and other giants. They don't have the financial constraints to overcome like we do but they have a lot of red tape and can't make decisions quickly like we can."

Cougar remains focused on just one product line, rather than many, "which gives us less diversification, but does allow us to be the experts, which benefits our customers," Allen says. That expertise enables Cougar to manufacture many specialized components used in the overhaul of Solar engines or turbines that customers can't get anywhere else.

Cougar's fast growth has been another restriction on the company's capital. Banks have been nervous that with contracts carrying such large price tags that the company is using its line of credit for operating capital instead of revolving purposes. "Bankers don't understand rapid growth like ours, and every year when our line of credit comes up for renewal we spend three weeks justifying what we do," Allen says. "You have to be very careful. It's hard to pull back on the reins, which entrepreneurs don't like to do, and not to grow too fast."

That challenge makes careful negotiation of contract terms with every supplier and customer all the more important for Cougar's continued financial strength.

58. GOOD PERFORMANCE SAVES MONEY

Companies with a good track record for completing jobs with
quality work, on time, and within budget receive financial
benefits as well as customer satisfaction.

■ ■ ■

From its first headquarters in a spare bedroom in 1984, Rowland Companies in Scottsdale, Arizona, has grown to annual revenues of $60 million and 73 employees. The general contractor and construction and development management company has a track record of excellence for constructing churches, medical facilities, and commercial buildings in 13 states from California to Texas to Wisconsin. Rowland Companies' motto—A Matter of Excellence—depends on doing a thousand things a little better than the rest.

That track record of completing work with excellence pays benefits beyond customers' praise. The construction industry relies on surety bonds. A third-party company ensures the customer that the contractor will fulfill all promises in the construction contract. Such bonding isn't free. On big projects it can cost tens of thousands of dollars, and the contractor builds that cost into its bid to do the work.

"You have to have some level of financial stability with a surety company to get someone to underwrite the bond," explains Brian Rowland, chief financial officer for Rowland Companies. "Most people would be shy to award very large construction contracts without bonds."

With two decades of performance history, Rowland Companies can easily demonstrate its ability to get bonding as well as an ability to do quality work on time and within budget.

"When you have a long track record of completing projects and when you're financially stable, customers see if they can waive the surety bonds," Brian says.

In such cases, the customer, who pays for the bond, weighs how much its risk increases versus the cost of the bond. If the risk is minimal, based on the contractor's history, the savings is substantial. And the contractor gets an edge in winning the contract by being able to knock thousands or tens of thousands of dollars off the bid.

A strong performance history can shave costs for many types of companies. It can result in lower interest rates on loans and credit cards, higher borrowing limits, better lease terms, return of security deposits on leased property, and discounts on purchases. The more companies save by demonstrating their quality and reliability, the less capital they need to raise and the more likely they are to secure capital when they need it.

In construction, the project owner doesn't waive the requirement for a surety bond lightly. Surety companies require a contractor to provide a list of good references and prove its experience in fulfilling the requirements of contracts in the past. The surety company also looks at the owner's personal assets outside the company, banking relationships, and lines of credit, which contractors use for short-term financing. All those factors and more must be in place for a customer to waive the bond.

The better a contractor's performance over the years, the less personal guarantee a surety company will require, Brian says. However, surety companies have gone bankrupt themselves by doing bonds without guarantees, and construction lenders often demand bonds on projects as a condition for obtaining a loan.

Even if Rowland Companies often works without surety bonds, it still maintains good relationships with bonding companies and bond underwriters, Brian stresses.

"We work with a bond broker who is very knowledgeable about the industry and the requirements of different surety companies," he says. "His commission is paid by the bond underwriter, so it's a free service to us. The underwriter comes out once a year to make sure we still meet its subjective measures. A company that can no longer meet the requirements will close its doors eventually because it won't be able to get bonding in the future. So it's important for Rowland Companies to maintain its high performance standards and track record."

59. BUSINESS INCUBATORS

Business support centers hatch new companies by providing
economical space, shared services, and free mentoring.

■ ■ ■

While still an undergraduate student at Union College in Schenectady, New York, Derek Mebus and a friend started building Internet portals for local government entities almost as a hobby in 2000. As the venture started growing, Derek needed to treat it like a real business and have a place to meet clients other than his dorm room. But he didn't have the resources for rent and other office necessities like desks and photocopiers.

An instructor told him to check out the U-Start business incubator. "There are two business incubators in Schenectady, and we didn't know about either of them," Derek says.

Business incubators started opening around the United States in the 1970s as a means to encourage entrepreneurial ventures to succeed, add jobs, and build local economies. There are hundreds across the country. Most are nonprofit entities, many associated with educational institutions or local economic development agencies, which give their fledging tenants below-market rents; shared services such as copiers, receptionist, and conference rooms; and free mentors and advisors. U-Start, for example, specializes in high-tech start-ups. The incubator is an independent nonprofit that is associated with Union College, which does not make direct contributions but does provide two buildings for very low rent and takes care of maintenance and security, says Executive Director Jon Lemelin. The incubator's operating revenues come from successful business leaders, banks, and foundations.

The capital savings and valuable free assistance can be the difference between success and failure for fledgling companies. Eighty-seven percent of firms that get their start in a business incubator survive, a much higher rate than start-ups in general, Jon says. And incubators create local jobs at about a tenth of the cost of public jobs programs.

Treetop Solutions moved into a nine-foot-by-nine-foot space in the U-Start incubator across the street from Union College. While the low cost was beneficial, Derek says, "We started realizing the real benefits after we moved in. They assigned us a mentor who understood our business and had good industry contacts. She helped us realize everything we needed to be a successful business."

Treetop Solutions also greatly benefited from quarterly meetings with Jon Lemelin at which Derek explained the company's progress on its goals, examined any goals not achieved, and set new goals for the next quarter.

"It gives you a sense of accountability," Derek says. "It allowed us to figure out what business we were really in."

Treetop Solutions quickly found that the portal part of the Internet was saturated and the company needed to identify a clearer niche. With the help of U-Start mentors and advisors, the company evolved to provide Web sites and online tools and services for small to mid-sized companies that don't have in-house information technology departments.

Treetop Solutions has grown so much that it moved out of U-Start but remains an affiliate eligible for the free mentoring and quarterly accountability meetings. It has six employees and some interns from the college.

"These high-tech companies not only provide their own jobs but their employees require a lot of subsequent services," Jon says. "They need restaurants, dry cleaners, retail stores. There's leverage that lifts the entire economy."

60. REHABILITATION SERVICES

Sheltered workshops and other services to provide jobs
and rehabilitation training for the disabled or injured can
provide workers and space for small businesses.

Dennis Myers is an industrial engineer with expertise in metal working who has jumped back and forth between corporate America and entrepreneurship throughout his career. After Dennis built up a division to grind and sharpen the extremely small drills used by the circuit board industry, his employer decided to drop the line of work. So Dennis started Facet Industries to do the job.

"I needed some minimum-experienced people and a place to locate the operation," Dennis says. "I worked out a deal with an agency that rehabilitated disabled and handicapped people in Mission Viejo, California. In exchange for my business employing some of their people, they provided free a facility and a supervisor, who was a college graduate, who aided in training the workers."

The rehabilitation agency didn't give Facet Industries capital, but gave space rent free and training supervision, saving the capital Facet Industries did have for other uses.

"All in all, it was worth thousands of dollars a month to me and a steady source of employees. They were some of my best employees and the most reliable," Dennis adds. "I paid the workers so I was providing jobs and training. That was the payoff for the rehabilitation agency."

Much of the work at Facet Industries was detailed and repetitive. The drills were the size of a pin, so grinding was detailed work. They needed to be cleaned and then shaped on a semi-automatic machine. Some of his workers were developmentally disabled but capable of doing the repetitious work under the tutelage of the supervisor.

"They worked hard and didn't have bad habits that some workers bring to the workplace," Dennis says. Some of his able-bodied workers would walk off the job after a couple of days never returning even to pick up their paycheck. In contrast, Dennis remembers one rehabilitation worker who learned to use a micrometer to check the size of each drill and sorted them into bins according to size. He never missed a day of work and sometimes even stood in the rain waiting for Dennis to open the doors.

Every state has state and federal funding to help reeducate and train people who are injured and can no longer work at the jobs they held prior to being injured and to train the physically and developmentally disabled. Most states have rehabilitation training centers and sheltered workshops and seek contracts with companies in the community that need assembly, sorting, collating of printed materials, labeling, and bulk mailing services. Some states permit below-minimum-wage jobs, paying the workers according to the labor they can do. For example, if a supervisor can assemble six chairs in an hour and the rehabilitation client can assemble one, then the client-worker earns a sixth the standard wage for that job. The workshops even market for the contracts, just as other private businesses would. Some rehabilitation specialists strive to have the training and jobs at sites in the community where a company's other employees work, so that the disabled have interaction with a broader cross-section of their neighbors.

After several years, Dennis closed Facet Industries and moved on to other executive industrial assignments and businesses. Today he's an executive coach and industrial consultant. He still says his rehabilitation workers were among the most reliable he ever had. "The biggest underutilized resource[s] in American business are the disabled and elderly workers," he says.

61. MOVE TO A LOWER-COST LOCATION

Some companies can save a substantial amount of money by
moving to locations with lower cost of living and taxes.

■ ■ ■

The Buck family has been making sport and utility knives since 1902, first in Kansas, then in San Diego, California, after World War II. It moved to El Cajon, California, in 1968. Its knives are considered the best quality on the market and hold a sharp edge longer because founder Hoyt Buck, a blacksmith apprentice, figured out a better way to temper steel. In January 2005, Buck Knives made its latest move to Post Falls, Idaho. The company estimates it is saving $1.2 million a year in the new location.

Business owners choose their location for many reasons: access to transportation, labor pool, or supplies; lifestyle or personal reasons; and proximity to customers. Cost is another major consideration. It certainly is a factor for Buck Knives, which has faced increasing overseas competition and demands from major retailers for lower-priced products. At the same time, costs of doing business had steadily increased in Southern California. Electricity prices skyrocketed in the early 2000s. Wages and other labor costs, such as workers compensation insurance, are among the highest in the United States. Everything from gasoline to land cost more in California than most other states.

"The major savings we can achieve in Idaho are hard to ignore in an increasingly competitive marketplace," says C.J. Buck, the company's chief executive and fourth generation family member in the business. "The simple truth is we can continue to achieve and surpass our goals more effectively in Idaho than in California."

Buck Knives, with annual revenues of $34 million, wants to continue to make its knives in the United States. However, it has moved 15 percent of its manufacturing overseas to be able to meet the prices demanded by retailers like Wal-Mart. Company officials are hopeful that production can be brought back to the Idaho plant. Salaries and cost of living are about 25 percent lower in northern Idaho than in Southern California. Workers compensation insurance and electricity are much lower in Idaho. The state has also provided incentives, including discounted land price for a 128,000-square-foot factory and $3,000 per employee in job training. Buck Knives brought 50 employees from El Cajon and hired 200 new employees in Idaho.

"The move gives us a chance for a new start, to bring in a new group of employees not indoctrinated in the old way of doing business," C.J. says. In response to customers buying less product but more often, Buck Knives has instituted lean manufacturing, which requires more teamwork and timing in manufacturing than the company formerly used. "Our reaction time is less predictable, so we need to be much more fast and flexible."

However, the move was not free. Buck Knives paid $800,000 for 12 acres and built a $7 million factory. "What surprised us, although it shouldn't have, was the cost of severance pay and relocation bonuses," C.J. says. "We let 200 people go and brought 50 people with us to train the new hires, and the total cost was $2 million."

C.J. estimates that Buck Knives will recoup the total costs of moving in two years. "It's been an educational process. Is it worth it? Ask me in a few years."

PART 4

ONGOING BUSINESS CAPITAL

■ ■ ■

After a business has a financial track record, capital resources open up that weren't available previously. The experienced company qualifies for a variety of loans and lines of credit, sometimes without the personal guarantee of the owner. Its borrowing capacity usually increases so it can acquire larger sums of capital. The more financially successful the company, the greater the resources it can tap. Many business owners grouse that capital sources only want to give them money when they don't need it.

Significantly, even longtime business owners continue to put their own money into their ventures in two ways. They reinvest profits and put up additional personal capital from time to time. They continue to use personal assets, such as their homes and life insurance, for business loans. They never outgrow the need to be frugal with the company's money or to use their ingenuity to obtain or maximize operating capital. As some of these chapters make clear, business owners occasionally lose sleep over their enterprise's capital needs even after years of experience and past successes. They consider what they can barter or sell to help the core business. Flexibility is vital. If one plan fails to raise adequate capital, secondary options must be considered.

As in Part 2, this section has examples of special or geographically specific programs offering business capital. Look around your industry or community for other similar programs for which your business qualifies.

If the company's track record warrants, it can attract more equity capital than it could in its formative stages, and eventually can access the stock market. The question arises whether those sources might cost more in terms of control than they're worth. Different owners answer that question differently.

YOU NEVER OUTGROW THE NEED OF SOME CAPITAL SOURCES

■ ■ ■

People who start businesses expect them to be not just profitable but to provide a good living for themselves and their families. The companies that survive do. However, the owners of those successful businesses generally do not consider every cent of profit to be their own salary. They reinvest profits and put additional personal capital into the business from time to time. They continue to use personal assets, such as their homes and life insurance, for business loans. They also continue to seek investments and loans from relatives and friends. In many cases, those friendly investors are participating in good companies with higher returns on investment than they can earn anywhere else.

62. PERSONAL FUNDS

Most businesses never outlive the need to rely on owners' personal funds to sustain operations and grow the company.

■ ■ ■

When Tony Welder chose a career, he looked for something in the medical field that also offered the prospect for business ownership. He worked for a pharmacy for six years after college and had a great relationship with his boss. But his job offered no ownership opportunity. So he quit to buy his own pharmacy in 1967 and has owned several over the years.

"With hard work the business grew. I bought another and that grew, etc.," Tony says. "That growth was usually financed with profits and bank loans."

Tony's history is common. Business owners who are successful over a long period do not take out every dime they can from their ventures. They continually retain some profits in the business to ensure healthy finances and fund growth. Greed and high living are factors that are certain to run a business into the ground.

In 1983, Tony bought Dakota Pharmacy in Bismarck, North Dakota. He had two employees.

"Business was not great, but I saw a huge potential because it was located in a clinic with more than 100 physicians," Tony says. "I was right, and the business quintupled in about two years."

One of Tony's strategies has always been to set some money aside for growth. "And don't be afraid to fail," he says. "You won't try anything new if you are afraid to fail."

In 1996, the clinic where Dakota Pharmacy was located wanted to own the pharmacy, so Tony had to find a new location. Some predicted he wouldn't survive six months.

"I moved to a stand-alone pharmacy with good parking close to the major health care facilities in Bismarck," Tony says. "We were able to market all over."

Dakota Pharmacy grew even larger. Again, by retaining profits and keeping good relationships with local banks, Tony built Dakota Pharmacy into more than a drugstore.

"It's about a lot more than dispensing prescriptions," he says. "We are thought of as innovators in the Bismarck area."

Dakota Pharmacy has a drive-through window. Its laboratory works with doctors to specially mix medications not available commercially and that are suited for the individual patient. The staff of 18 nurses, pharmacists, and a naturopathic physician does health screenings for blood pressure and glucose, bone mineral density testing for osteoporosis, testing for cholesterol, body fat, cardio-vision, and more. Customers can refill prescriptions online. The company has a commitment not just to treat patients who are sick but to do everything possible to keep customers healthy.

A commitment of personal time and money are always required in business. "So I had less money for discretionary spending, but just put money back into growth of that business or into a new business," Tony says. "I didn't drive the most expensive car or have the most expensive house. My family lived well, though. I'm pretty conservative so the material, showy things aren't real important."

Tony now has ownership interest in five pharmacies. And the personal commitment of time and money continues unabated.

63. PROFITS FROM THE BUSINESS

Once a business starts generating revenue, the owner must set aside some of that capital for unanticipated needs and growth.

■ ■ ■

Larry Wickkiser says he has two keys to the success of his company, Wickkiser International Companies in Ferndale, Washington. "I hired a very frugal person to be the general manager, and I married a very frugal person. My tendency is to spend all the money I have, a consequence of hasty decision making," he says. "But my general manager has chief financial officer experience, and he's continually telling me, 'If you want to spend X amount of money on this, you won't have money for that.'"

Wickkiser International is the parent company for Airporter Shuttle, which provides daily bus service to and from the Seattle-Tacoma International Airport, and Bellair Charters, which leases motor coaches, minibuses, vans, and limousines to groups of all sizes for trips throughout the Northwest and Canada. In 1993, Larry took over the company started by his father in 1985. The business survived the start-up phase because of his father's persistence, but for the long term, Larry recognized the importance of a strong financial hand on the company because the most significant source of operating capital for an existing business is the business itself.

Virtually every surviving business uses its own resources for operations and growth. In the first place, no business owner can calculate every potential expense. He needs a slush fund for unexpected occurrences and opportunities. Some of the most successful smal business owners pride themselves on being able to pay for new equipment and expansion out of their own pocket. That habit avoids diminishing the owner's equity. Even if the business seeks loans or equity investment from outsiders, those capital providers typically insist that the owner also put capital into any project.

Perhaps the most common mistake new business owners make is to pay themselves a salary equal to the firm's profits. Those businesses often fail when the economy goes sour or tragedy strikes.

"We can take some, but then there always needs to be some money set aside," Larry says, "because we don't know when the lean years are coming, so we save. Our policy is to spend frugally and save the rest."

Larry doesn't have a specific percentage of revenues that he saves for the lean years. It is a greater amount in strong years and perhaps none in weak years.

The terrorist attacks of 2001 introduced a lean time for companies dependent on air transportation and tourism as Wickkiser International does in part. Although the company had contracts for event shuttles and public transportation, that work wasn't enough to completely make up the revenues lost when air transportation dropped dramatically.

"The airlines ran to the government to bail them out, but it wasn't bailing out bus companies," Larry says. "If we were totally reliant on tourism, we would be in trouble."

Wickkiser International has continually added buses and services, such as seasonal transportation to Seattle Mariners baseball games and Seahawks football games and regular routes into downtown Seattle. The company carried its one millionth passenger in 2003.

"We have achieved that success because I hire people who balance my character traits and weaknesses and help me manage and plan financially," Larry says.

64.

FAMILY

Even after the start-up phase, relatives are a
source of capital to sustain and grow a company.

■ ■ ■

Sharon Bennett managed to launch Premier Pet Products in Rich-
mond, Virginia, in 1989 with a $5,000 personal loan from a bank because
she had strong personal credit. She started making and selling special dog
collars. However, over the next several years, as Premier Pet Products
grew, Sharon turned to her mother and father for capital.

Her mother, June Madere, loaned the company $100,000 that she was
saving for her retirement.

"She loaned us money when no one else would," Sharon says. "We
paid a higher interest rate on the money but paid her interest only, which
helped cash flow. It was a good deal for her because she earned more interest than she would have gotten from other investments."

Premier Pet Products still has that loan on the books and continues to
pay interest only, which provides ongoing income for June.

The company has grown to more than a hundred employees and more
than $10 million in annual sales, adding creative, fun, and fashionable pet
products, such as the Gentle Leader head collar, Fido Fleece apparel, and
KeepSafe Break-Away collar. The company was founded by pet people,
hires pet lovers, and is committed to providing safe, humane, unique, and
effective tools that help improve the relationship between customers and
their pets.

"This has a happy ending because the company is so successful, but
that was high risk for her putting up her retirement money," Sharon says.
"I felt confident about the business, but still it was a risk. If I had lost
Mom's money, it would have put a strain on our relationship."

Experts advise structuring any loan or equity investment from family
with a written agreement that details when and how repayment will be
made. The risk should be even more clearly stated than for nonrelatives,
especially if it is an equity investment. Resist the urge to believe Mom or
Dad when they say, "You don't have to pay me back." A moral commit-

ment to repaying that obligation has spurred many entrepreneurs to success through insurmountable odds.

June was not the only relative to step up to help Premier Pet Products grow. In 2001, the company wanted to acquire another business and needed to raise $300,000 in two weeks for a down payment. Sharon's father, Sherman Madere, and partner Evan Wooten's parents loaned money to close the deal. Again, Premier Pet Products structured the loans as three-year, interest-only notes, which helped cash flow, and paid off the principal amount at the end of three years.

"If you have investors who want a continuing income stream, interest-only loans are the way to go," Sharon says. "It also benefits the company to maximize cash flow as much as possible."

Sharon recommends caution when asking family members for business capital.

"Don't borrow from your family money that they can't afford to lose, because it might not work out, and that can affect relationships forever," she says. "If you ask, give them an easy out if they are not comfortable giving you money. Make sure they know there will be no hard feelings if they say no, if they are not comfortable with the risk level."

65. FRIENDS

Even established companies often turn to friends
when a need for capital arises.

■ ■ ■

Elaine Martin had been in the business of providing fencing, guardrails, and concrete barriers for highways in Nampa, Idaho, for nine years when everything seemed to go wrong at once. In 1995 she divorced and needed to pay off a great number of debts in order to keep her business, MarCon Inc. She was hospitalized with health problems. Her partner decided to retire, and Elaine needed to buy out his 49 percent ownership of the company.

"I wanted to own as much of the company as I could, so I sold 11 percent of the company to a friend who lived in Colorado in order to have the capital I needed," Elaine says. "With all those things going wrong at once, I did need the money, but in a year I would grow the company so that I wouldn't. Several years later [the investor] became my significant other, so that worked out well."

As noted in Chapter 16, family and friends are among the most common sources for start-up capital. When Elaine started MarCon her mother put up a $25,000 certificate of deposit to secure a business loan. But as Elaine's later experience shows, the value of friends and family doesn't end when the company matures. The people who know you best are the most likely to believe in your business strategies enough to put their own money on the line. Even though MarCon was an established company doing highway work in Oregon, Nevada, and Utah as well as Idaho, it was small in 1995. Elaine knew she could grow the company and make it a good investment for her friend.

"Looking back I see that everything I did was entrepreneurial, but I never thought about my work in those terms," Elaine says. "It was just a financial necessity."

Some business owners take advantage of friends who help their companies financially. They put off repayment of loans or ignore friends' roles as equity investors. Elaine was careful to spell out the terms of her friend's investment in MarCon. "We had a very definite buy-sell agreement," she says. "With 30 days' notice he could get his money or I could [unilaterally] buy his stock. That's the way you keep friends. You make clear what the outcomes will be if it doesn't work out. You have to be able to know what their needs and expectations are."

Entrepreneurs who involve their family or friends in business must be extremely careful, Elaine adds. Each side must understand the risk, the potential profits, and the long-term expectations of the other. "Too many people make the mistake of not having an up-front agreement about what is going to happen," she says. "They also need to be careful who they deal with. I would not have taken start-up financial help from anyone other than my mother, and I would not have asked any of my other friends to invest in my company when I needed help in 1995."

MarCon now has annual revenues of $3 million to $8 million, depending on the amount of road construction in her four-state market. She has 20 to 40 employees at any given time. "I've had slow, steady growth because I have put everything back into the business."

SECTION B

EXPANDED LOAN OPTIONS

■ ■ ■

Once a business has survived the start-up phase, it has more possibilities and programs for borrowing capital. Financial institutions that won't look at a business less than two years old become advisors and lending partners for more established firms. Vendors and equipment providers are also more willing to work with a company that has staying power. The payment terms become more favorable and product choices expand. Even the company's own receivables become assets for capital and loans.

66. HOME EQUITY LOAN

Because a house is the biggest asset many people own, some
business owners tap the equity in that personal asset for
capital at some point in the life of their companies.

■ ■ ■

After selling business forms as an employee for five years, Bill Houghton and a friend pooled their client lists to start Horizon Business Systems in Las Vegas, Nevada, in 1992. The company has grown to 13 employees and ownership of its own 8,500-square-foot building. Revenues are six times larger than in the initial year. As continuous-roll business forms became obsolete, Horizon Business Systems added corporate attire, advertising specialties, trophies, and labels. "Companies use millions and millions of labels each year," Bill says. "There are 26 labels inside one computer alone."

After Bill's partner left to pursue a career as a full-time professional poker player—a gamble even a former gold prospector like Bill wouldn't take—Bill was solely responsible for the financial health of the company.

Twice he pulled equity out of his own home to keep Horizon Business Systems growing and to help cash flow.

Tapping home equity is one of the most common sources of financing a U.S. business. A home is the largest asset many Americans have, and most real estate steadily appreciates in value in most economies, providing a pool of capital an entrepreneur can access fairly easily. Generally, the entrepreneur can get a lower interest rate, longer repayment term, and more money from a home equity loan than from a standard business loan. In fact, many business owners cannot qualify for other types of loans. However, a home equity loan for business purposes shouldn't be taken without study because business ownership is not risk free. The owner is basically putting the American dream of home ownership on the line for another American dream, business ownership. If your outstanding mortgage is 80 percent or more of the house's market value, many experts advise against pulling the remaining equity out to put into a business. Before taking a home equity loan, decide how you will use the money in your business. Calculate how much that usage will increase monthly revenues. If that increase at least covers your higher mortgage payment, the plan is probably sound.

Two different times Bill took this action to raise between $30,000 and $50,000 for Horizon Business Systems.

"You have to give everything you've got to make a business successful," Bill says. "If that means you take your biggest asset—in my case it's my home—then you do it."

Once Bill went to a mortgage company to refinance his house in order to get a lower interest rate and pull cash out. The other time, Bill went to investment manager Merrill Lynch & Co. to get cash and a lower monthly payment by tying the lower, adjustable interest rate to LIBOR, the London Interbank Offered Rate Index, which is the average of interest rates that major international banks charge each other to borrow U.S. dollars.

Neither Bill nor his wife, Jenny, worries about tapping home equity for the business.

"My wife trusts me implicitly; that makes all the difference," Bill says. "As long as I'm comfortable with it, she trusts me."

People who are confident taking the educated risks of running a business are different from employees. "One of my long-time employees calls it insanity," Bill says. "Everyone wants security but it comes through different avenues. If I had to sell both my houses to keep the business going, I'd do it."

67. BORROW AGAINST LIFE INSURANCE POLICY

A business owner may be able to borrow against the paid-up
cash value of a life insurance policy to obtain capital for
requirements of a start-up or ongoing company.

■ ■ ■

In the late 1970s, Steve Birge was working in Vermont restaurants so he could spend his free time skiing. He noticed that the restaurants needed fresh produce. So he approached fellow skier Mark Curran to join him in starting Black River Produce, which is now headquartered in Proctorsville, Vermont. They pooled some cash and got a loan for a Volkswagen bus to pick up fresh fruits and vegetables from the Boston wholesale market two-and-a-half hours away and transport them back to Vermont ski resorts.

"I wanted to get in to something that was a constant need," Steve says. "Everyone has to eat. Produce is good for you. The government gives you free advertising about the value of eating fruits and vegetables. This was something I saw as a great need."

The partnership provided shared leadership to run and grow Black River Produce. It also laid the foundation for a future source of capital because of the way Steve and Mark created their partnership. They wrote a buy-sell agreement, a contract that dictates how one partner can buy out the ownership of another. Most partnerships fail to take this simple step, which can cause trouble in the future even if the partners get along fine and the business prospers.

"You have to have a buy-sell agreement; it spells everything out clearly," Steve says.

One of the key issues of a buy-sell agreement is how to pay off the departing partner. Trying to pull money out of profits can cripple the company. The Black River Produce partners used a common technique of buying life insurance policies for each man that would provide the buyout money if one partner became disabled or died. Such policies build cash value, which can provide capital for the company even during the life of the partnership.

The Black River Produce partnership has been a tremendous success. They bring produce from all over the world to more than a thousand restaurants, schools, hospitals, and camps in Vermont, New Hampshire, and Massachusetts. They also take the locally grown produce to market in Boston. When Steve and Mark wanted to add a 10,000-square-foot warehouse, instead of obtaining a bank loan, they borrowed against the cash value in those partnership life insurance policies.

"We still have to pay it back, but this is our money, we don't pay interest on it," Steve says.

In many cases, if you have a whole life insurance policy, you can borrow from the insurance company, using the cash value of your insurance as collateral. Term life insurance doesn't provide such an option. The interest rate is significantly lower than for a typical bank loan. The insurance contract spells out how much can be borrowed. By using the cash value in the life insurance policies, Black River Produce's expansion project cost less. However, if the insured person dies before repaying the loan, the value of the insurance policy decreases and the death benefit is lower. The cash needed for the buy-sell agreement might not be available. Partners using this capital should weigh the risk and circumstances. Steve says he and his partner weren't concerned.

Black River Produce has been growing at 10 percent a year and now has 150 employees and a 60,000-square-foot distribution center. It hauls two tractor trailers loaded with produce from Boston each day.

"We started with nothing; now we're the biggest in the state," Steve says. "Growth was easy. Directing 150 people, that's hard."

68. BANK LINE OF CREDIT

An established, profitable business can use a line of credit to get through the peaks and valleys of short-term cash needs.

■ ■ ■

Chris Mott has been around tiny things his entire life. His grandmother collected Cracker Jack prizes from the age of eight and his grandfather carved pieces of furniture the size of a child's finger in the 1930s.

The Motts opened Mott's Miniatures in Los Angeles, California, in 1949. By the time Chris joined the doll house furniture and accessories retail shop in the late 1980s, it was in Buena Park. More recently it moved to a Fullerton, California, industrial park having moved most of its sales to mail order and the Internet. Mott's Miniatures experiences wide swings in revenues, depending on the economy and time of year. Chris smoothes that fluctuation with a $50,000 line of credit with a major bank. "I have used it for inventory purchases but mostly for cash flow needs," Chris says.

A bank line of credit is one of the most common forms of financing used by established companies. Most banks won't establish such a line until a business has been open two to three years. Some lenders require collateral, such as real estate or accounts receivable or even inventory. Chris doesn't have to provide any tangible security, but he does have to sign his personal guarantee for the line of credit, even though Mott's Miniatures is a corporation with more than a half-century of track record.

"Incorporation did nothing for me," Chris says. "Maybe banks are tougher on retailers, but they never would accept Motts Miniatures as a legal entity without personal guarantees."

A line of credit gives a business the flexibility to borrow to meet short-term financing needs, such as taking advantage of trade discounts, paying for unexpected expenses, or managing the seasonal ebbs and flows of revenue. Some businesses never tap their line of credit but pay an annual fee for the security of having it "just in case." Others use it for all sorts of purchases, such as equipment, that would more appropriately be put into some other kind of loan.

"I think it's important to use credit carefully," Chris says. "Business owners can go overboard with credit. I only use the line for short-term needs and pay it off as soon as I can. I don't think of it as a continual loan. When I have positive cash flow, I pay it off."

If he doesn't use the line of credit for a while, Chris's bank sends enticements to use it more frequently. "It's not interested in the amount of the line of credit; it wants interest payments, which can be a lot."

Some companies need much larger lines of credit than others, depending on expenses, revenues, age of receivables, and other factors. For example, a business with $1 million in sales annually has $2,740 in sales per day. If customers typically pay in 30 days, the business needs an $82,200 line of credit. Actually, the need is a little less because the company does have some profits in that cash flow. However, if more than half the sales come in December, which is not that rare for retailers, the line may need to be larger.

"When you own a small business, you do everything and anything you can to keep it going," Chris says. "The smaller you are, the more active you are in looking for every way to reduce expenses or wring that extra penny of profit."

69. REGULAR SBA LOANS

Many banks won't loan money to small businesses
without the federal government guarantee under
a variety of SBA programs.

■ ■ ■

Charles Keller was an industrial designer who started making custom furniture in his North Andover, Massachusetts, garage in the early 1970s. Driven by the demand of family and friends, the business grew until Charlie incorporated C.W. Keller & Associates in 1976. The company, which specializes in distinctive wood and custom wood-veneer products for retail, commercial, and residential customers, moved to Plaistow, New Hampshire, in 1989.

The company grew with the help of three different loans guaranteed by the U.S. Small Business Administration (SBA). Charlie witnessed first-hand the evolution of the loan program that Congress initiated as capital of last resort for small businesses who could not borrow any other way. The program has grown into the source of 30 percent of long-term loans to small businesses today. The SBA's largest loan program is called 7(a), which encompasses several special-interest loans with various requirements, such as microloans, employee stock ownership plans, pollution control, and export working capital loans.

Charlie's first SBA loan for equipment in 1979 went directly through the federal agency. "At that point the agency made direct loans. The SBA was the only way I could get the money," he says. "The bureaucracy was ridiculous. It took three months and six inches of paperwork to get the loan."

The SBA also required, as a condition of the loan, for borrowers to meet with business counselors from the Service Corps of Retired Executives (SCORE), which Charlie says was most helpful.

His second loan five years later was for more machinery and carried a lower interest rate than any other loan available.

By the time Charlie got his third SBA loan in the 1990s, the agency was no longer making direct loans but guaranteed loans made by private lenders. The change made possible many more loans because the federal government only had to pay lenders for loans on which the borrowers defaulted. In the 2004 fiscal year, 80,000 U.S. businesses borrowed $12.5 billion through SBA-guaranteed loans. As of 2005, loan defaults of an estimated $79 million are paid by fees on each loan.

The loan process has also changed dramatically, Charlie says. His banker of many years approached him and offered the $300,000 loan to expand his manufacturing facility. Charlie didn't have to fill out any paperwork. All he had to provide to obtain the 15-year, fixed-rate loan was company financial statements.

Many banks won't loan money at all to small businesses except through the SBA programs. The interest rates may be higher than that of standard loans. Also, the SBA requires that anyone who owns at least 20 percent of the borrowing company must also give a personal guarantee on the loan. One primary advantage is that SBA loans can have longer payback periods than standard loans. The loan requirements are set by the private lenders who participate in the program. Some are very friendly to small and young companies; others are not. Some loan only to franchises. Most lenders require the business to be two to three years old and profitable. Most want the borrower to put some money into the project for which the loan proceeds will be used. The program is certainly not for destitute entrepreneurs working on a dream.

But the SBA's loan program has helped C.W. Keller & Associates grow and prosper, Charlie says. The company has 35 employees, a 30,000-square-foot factory and $5 million in annual sales.

70.   SBA 504 LOANS

One government-guaranteed loan helps small businesses
buy real estate or equipment with a low down
payment and below-market interest rates.

■ ■ ■

Dave Winner had no idea what a hot business he was starting in 1989 when he opened Fabtech, a Southern California fabrication shop specializing in designing and building custom off-road suspension systems for two-wheel-drive trucks. Soon, young drivers were coming to Dave for custom-made trucks. He developed a system for using the same frame with different accessories and parts for these built-to-order trucks. Within the first year Fabtech moved from its original, leased 1,000-square-foot space to 2,500 square feet, and then Dave started leasing additional nearby buildings.

By 1998, Dave decided that owning a building was a better use of Fabtech's capital than leasing, so he wanted to buy a 20,000-square-foot building in Brea, California. His commercial real estate broker told him he needed a 504 loan.

"I didn't even know what that was," Dave says. "I got this stack of paperwork a mile high, and I told my broker that I couldn't do it; I had a business to run."

The 504 loan program under the U.S. Small Business Administration (SBA) is designed to create jobs and build the local economy. A small business can use it to buy fixed assets such as real estate and equipment. It's attractive for the business because the down payment and interest rate may be lower than a regular commercial real estate loan. With a 504 loan, a commercial lender typically picks up 50 percent of the purchase price, the borrowing company 10 percent, and a certified development company (CDC) the remaining 40 percent. The SBA periodically bundles the 504 loans and sells debentures on them to private investors. On the down side, the maximum CDC portion is $1.3 million, and the 504 loan has a prepayment penalty for the first ten years, so it's not a good deal for big projects or companies that move every year.

Dave says one of the greatest benefits is working with the trained staff of the CDC, which in his case was Southland Economic Development Corp. in Santa Ana, California. Its staffers did most of the loan application paperwork for him.

"It was scary," Dave remembers. "I had 12 employees at the time, and Robert Dodge with Southland said, 'In a year, you'll have 30 employees.' I said, 'Whoa!' But within a year I had 50 employees."

Fabtech outgrew that building within 15 months and leased the 30,000-square-foot building next door. Eighteen months later it needed more space. This time, Dave decided to buy five acres in nearby Chino, California, and build a 100,000-square-foot plant. The $6.5 million project exceeded the 504 loan maximum and Dave didn't want to pay the prepayment penalty on his previous 504-financed building. So when the Brea building was sold, instead of paying off the 504 loan, it was transferred to the new project, plus Southland made another 504 loan so that the two totaled the maximum allowable $1.3 million. Fabtech made its 10 percent down payment, and the lender made a larger-than-usual loan.

The 504 loan program is a good way for a company like Fabtech to conserve cash for running and growing the business, Dave says. In fact, Fabtech has been able to add more jobs and boost the economy even more than it had earlier. It now has 250 employees and has spilled into the 40,000-square-foot building next door.

71. FEDERAL ECONOMIC INJURY DISASTER LOAN

Storms and earthquakes aren't the only disasters for which
small businesses can qualify for government-guaranteed
loans to rebuild damaged business property.

■ ■ ■

Ten days before Christmas 2001 a gas-fired portable water heater misfired in the basement of the historic Tisbury Inn in Vineyard Haven on Martha's Vineyard, Massachusetts. Fire quickly gutted the 200-year-old hotel. Smoke and water damaged the adjacent Zephrus restaurant. Besides the inn's historic importance to the small community, its destruction left a blemish on the island's main street from the ferry.

Owners Susan and Sherman Goldstein were torn about rebuilding. They did not have enough insurance to cover such extensive damage because the inn had fire sprinklers and the fire station was across the street, Susan says. "No one imagined the whole thing would burn down."

Still, Sherman adds, "We have lived here for more than 30 years. We have a special responsibility to employees, business neighbors, and other residents of the town."

Fortunately for the Goldsteins, Massachusetts Congressman William Delahunt immediately assigned one of his staff members to find help and support for rebuilding the inn. Because of the inn's prominent location and economic importance to Martha's Vineyard, it was declared a federal disaster area, which made it eligible for government guaranteed disaster loans. Those loans gave the Goldsteins working capital to keep key employees and pay operating expenses during the 18 months the inn was closed.

Businesses that qualify for disaster loans can get below-market interest rates for loans to replace personal and real property as well as working capital. The program, which channels through the Federal Emergency Management Agency, is best known for helping rebuild areas struck by hurricanes, floods, earthquakes, and other natural disasters.

In the Goldsteins' case, private lenders also stepped up. Local politicians, normally tough on developers, approved permits and plans for the long-time Vineyard residents that outsiders might not receive, Sherman says. Still, that assistance did not make the process swift or easy. The Goldsteins applied for every loan and assistance program for which they might possibly be eligible. No single one was large enough to cover the entire rebuilding cost.

"The amount of paperwork we had with the insurance, banks, and legal issues was enormous, the U.S. Small Business Administration (which administers federal disaster loans) really stood out as remarkably efficient," Sherman says. "As the loan applications wended through various offices, I don't recall being asked the same question twice. Every person I dealt with was well-versed in the circumstances around our situation."

The town would not allow the Goldsteins to add more rooms to the inn's original 32 during the reconstruction. So they needed to expand and upgrade the project, adding a spa and resort-quality rooms to justify higher prices sufficient to cover the costs of the loans. In many ways, the rebuilt hotel, which the Goldsteins returned to its original name Mansion House, was like a new business.

"The inn was very successful and at the point immediately before the fire, Susie and I were virtually retired," Sherman says. "Some of our staff and the general manager had been with us since 1985. Susie was not working a lot, and I came in at 9:00 AM and by 2:00 I was thinking how I could leave."

"The fire changed that. I'm here at 6:30 in the morning and don't go home until after dark, seven days a week," he says. "We worked very, very hard when we first bought it in 1985 and we're working very, very hard now."

72. VENDOR LINE OF CREDIT

Product suppliers often provide favorable credit terms
to customer companies, which must honor purchase
contracts in order to retain the vendors' trust.

■ ■ ■

After struggling as an independent brick-and-mortar retailer in the early 1990s, Daniel Thralow in 1996 discovered the power of the Internet, which was then in its infancy. He set up a text-only site as an experiment to promote his sunglasses-only store in Duluth, Minnesota, and started getting orders from all over the country. But Dan was getting about 10 percent of the sunglasses back from customers who didn't like the product when they put the sunglasses on, so he added nonwearable products, such as binoculars and telescopes, which had a return rate of just 3 percent. By 1999, Thralow Inc. was selling $3.5 million in products, mostly through http://www.peepers.com, http://www.binoculars.com, and http://www.telescopes.com, and made the *Inc.* magazine list of 500 fastest growing privately owned companies in America. Product suppliers were willing to give Dan merchandise and wait as long as 180 days to be paid without charging any interest.

"The dollar amount and length of time they extend varies," Dan says, "but even a young company that can sit down with vendors and explain how it will sell product will get at least 30 days to pay for $3,000 or $5,000 in merchandise. And if you do well selling their product, there's no reason not to increase the terms. We would not have grown as fast as we did without vendor lines of credit."

Dan sold his company in 1999 for cash and stock in the buying company, which went bankrupt following the dot-com crash. In 2001 Dan got his company back along with a bad reputation among vendors who had not been paid.

"I had to fly out and visit vendors in person," Dan says. "I offered to pay cash on delivery just to keep their products, and some still didn't want to do business with me even though I reminded them that I had paid on time when I was in charge of the company."

Dan had to establish new relationships with other vendors to wipe away the tarnished reputation and prove himself and Thralow Inc. worthy of vendors' trust and lines of credit. Slowly he has been able to win back all the former vendors. Even so, some companies harbor hard feelings. "I order $1 million in product from one company, and they still sting from and bring up the $30,000 they were not paid in 2000. It is said that customers are golden, and they are. But your suppliers are just as golden. Some products sell themselves because of their brand name. You have to be good to those suppliers and keep your word."

Thralow Inc. now has 25 employees. In addition to its own Internet retail sites, the company links its database of 33,000 products to 11 sites owned by others whose primary products complement Thralow binoculars and telescopes, such as outdoor clothing. Thralow Inc. provides the call centers and order fulfillment for these other sites, which maximizes the use of Thralow's staff and warehouse space, multiplies sales, and helps control retail prices for the products. These other small Internet sites benefit from Dan's success in rebuilding relationships with hundreds of vendors and rely on his ability to keep generous lines of credit with these vendors by delivering on his promises.

73. EQUIPMENT LEASING

Young companies that cannot qualify for regular loans can
usually lease equipment to preserve capital.

■ ■ ■

All Season Photography had been open just a year in Placentia, California, when owner Matt Breneman wanted to obtain digital photography equipment in order to expand his business. Banks wouldn't loan him the money until he had been in business two or three years and wanted substantial collateral or down payment. Matt didn't have enough money to buy the equipment outright and wanted to retain as much money as possible for operating capital. So he obtained $25,000 worth of cameras, printers, and software by leasing them.

Equipment leasing is basically renting rather than buying. At the end of the lease term, the user, called the lessee, can return the equipment or buy it. Leasing has become a huge factor in American businesses' ongoing challenge to make the best use of capital and protect cash flow while growing. Eighty-five percent of U.S. companies lease equipment—ranging from medical diagnostic machinery to cameras—and spend about $218 billion a year, according to the Equipment Leasing Association in Virginia. These companies use equipment leasing to manage growth and assets, keep state-of-the-art machinery, and increase cash flow. "My business didn't have any payment history, so the leasing broker used my personal credit history," Matt says. "The first lease helped All Season Photography establish its creditworthiness.

"Still, with the initial lease, I took a huge risk in my business because I was going from film to digital technology," Matt says. He wanted to expand his market to include school events and sports photography to the standard portrait photography capabilities in his business. If the leased equipment did not deliver quality products, it would damage All Season Photography's reputation.

A business owner should consider, as Matt did, how the equipment will build the business. It ought to increase revenues and help the company achieve planned goals.

Matt agreed to a five-year lease, but digital camera technology has changed so rapidly that some of the leased equipment was obsolete before the term was up. When Matt leased a second camera, he obtained a three-year term. "For some equipment it wouldn't matter," he says. "A lens can stay in service 15 years, so there's no reason not to put it on a longer lease."

In some cases, equipment can be leased with no money down. If it is an operating lease, rather than a capital lease—ask your accountant—it doesn't show up on financial statements as debt. That accounting detail can boost the company's financial health. However, you still should be honest with your banker if you are leasing equipment. Your company can deduct the lease as an overhead expense on tax returns, whereas with a loan, only the interest portion is deductible while the value of the equipment is depreciated over several years.

Leasing does have some drawbacks. Most manufacturers and brokers won't do leases on equipment that costs just a few hundred dollars. Also, leasing costs more than an outright purchase. The interest rate will vary depending on the type of equipment, lessee's credit rating, length of the lease, and current cost of money.

And business owners need to shop around and be wary of unregulated leasing companies, Matt says. He always has his accountant review lease documents. The lessee should watch for hidden fees or a last-minute increase in the interest rate when the final lease agreement is drawn up. Look for added costs at the end of the lease. Find out who is responsible if the leased equipment is damaged or destroyed.

74. FACTORING

Selling accounts receivable can help cash flow for fast-growing
or young companies, but the cost of capital is steep.

■ ■ ■

Erick Barnett started Advance Med LLC in Cedar Park, Texas, September 1, 2001. The company, which provides professional radiology specialists and registered nurse anesthetists, was growing rapidly. Erick often needed to pay his staff before the hospital and medical center clients paid him. However, following the terrorist attacks in New York City and Washington, D.C., shortly after Erick opened the door, the loan and capital markets dried up, and Erick didn't want to accept help offered by relatives.

Companies like Advance Med that sell products or services on time can sell their accounts receivable to a third party, called a factor. The factor buys the accounts receivable based on the creditworthiness of the customer, so even start-ups like Advance Med can use this method to smooth out cash flow even if they can't qualify for a bank loan or other forms of financing.

"We bill the health facility for the services of our radiology technicians and nurses but we don't get paid for 45 days or so," Erick says. With factoring, "we get our money immediately so we can pay our people."

However, factoring is expensive, Erick cautions. "I think we were paying 3 percent or 4 percent a month. It was ridiculous. We slowly got out of it within a year."

The monthly interest isn't the only cost. While the factor pays the accounts receivable seller within a day or two, it gives only a percentage of the face value of the receivables, which varies by industry. Factors might pay 70 percent to a clothing manufacturer but only 50 percent to a medical clinic. They may tack on other charges, such as auditing fees, collateral maintenance fees, or up-front points. Factors tend to specialize in certain industries. Ask your banker or other business owners in your industry to recommend a reputable factor.

Many factors require a company to sell all their receivables for six months to a year and have a minimum of $5,000 or more monthly. But Erick said Advance Med was able to use its factor as much or as little as the personnel agency needed. Still, Advance Med kept its costs low to build a financial cushion so that it could stop factoring as quickly as possible. The company now provides staff to 40 hospitals a month and has multiyear contracts with Veterans Administration facilities. Advance Med has been on *Entrepreneur* magazine's list of 100 fastest growing companies two different years.

The average company that uses factoring stops the practice in favor of lower-cost lines of credit or other financing within three to four years of start-up. Some will use factoring periodically, depending on the economy and other circumstances, such as a period of fast growth that outstrips the company's savings and lines of credit or seasonal fluctuations in sales. A few continue to use factoring regularly, building the costs into their pricing just as they do the cost of accepting credit card payments. Small firms that don't have in-house collections departments find the factor's collection services valuable. Also, factors are experts at checking customers' credit. If a factor won't accept the receivables of one of your clients, maybe you shouldn't either.

75. RECEIVABLES AS COLLATERAL FOR A LOAN

You don't necessarily have to sell receivables to get capital.
Lenders may accept them as security for a loan or line of credit.

■ ■ ■

Since 1973, South Texas Vocational Technical Institute has been providing private, post–high school training, first in English as a second language and now short-term career training. It starts and graduates students every six weeks in programs such as medical or legal office skills, pharmacy technician, and childcare and development. While the education industry fluctuates with the economy, South Texas Vo-Tech has about 1,000 students at any one time at campuses in McAllen, Brownsville, and Weslaco, Texas, and graduates about 90,000 people annually. As a federally accredited school, it receives federal student aid to help pay tuition and other program costs. For the past ten years, the school has used its accounts receivable from students and federal aid as collateral for bank lines of credit, says Rosanna Ferguson, the chief financial officer whose parents founded the school under the name Texas Language Academy.

Borrowing against the value of accounts receivable is one of the cheapest financing options available to a company, which often gets a better interest rate than banks give their best customers for regular commercial loans. Borrowing against the receivables—either through a bank or an asset-based lender—is about half the cost of selling them outright to a factor. This form of financing is particularly useful to companies like South Texas Vo-Tech whose day-to-day operational costs swell at certain times of the year, or those that cannot get other types of financing.

Receivables financing allows a company to get capital without taking on term debt or giving up equity. And the value of the receivables remains on the borrower's financial statement so the company is free to seek other types of business loans. However, unlike factoring, the borrower still has the responsibility to collect the money, so it's not a trouble-free source of capital. Also, an asset-based loan takes longer to get than capital from a factor because the lender wants to see audited financial statements and review the borrower's creditworthiness; whereas factors look at the creditworthiness of the customers of the borrower.

South Texas Vo-Tech is a growing company with 140 employees, which helps the school qualify for receivables financing, says Rosanna, who has worked in the company since she was five years old, starting with the simplest chores and working up through the ranks. A company must "prove itself to financial institutions; they are betting [through their lines of credit] that you are going to come through."

When South Texas Vo-Tech started using its receivables as collateral for lines of credit, the bank also insisted on personal guarantees from the owners, Rosanna says. "We don't have to put up personal guarantees any more because of our track record and length of time in business."

When shopping for receivables financing, it pays to shop around for more than just interest rate. Some lenders will only advance 70 percent of the face value of a company's quality receivables while others will advance 85 percent. The advance varies by industry as well as credit history. Some lenders tack on up-front points, audit fees, and collateral-maintenance fees, all of which add to the cost of the financing. Some offer lower interest rates if the company is willing to commit to the loan for a longer time.

76. EQUIPMENT DISTRIBUTOR

When banks won't finance equipment purchases,
the product sellers often will.

■ ■ ■

After losing their jobs from the same employer in 1993, Bill Hall and Steve Burd opened Action Mold, in Anaheim, California, a maker of custom, precision injection molds. Bill handled the customers and the books; Steve was the mold-making genius who decided what equipment to buy. The partners weren't shy about investing in equipment that would build their company. After two years, sales were $500,000 and Steve identified a $40,000 computer numerical control (CNC) machine from Haas Automation as the next must-have purchase. Action Mold had $20,000 on hand, so Bill went shopping for a loan for the rest.

"I went to six banks, including the one we had our business accounts with, and they all turned me down," Bill says. "Even my mother turned me down."

"My bank had a big sign in the lobby: 'We make small-business loans.' But the loan officer said the amount was so small it wouldn't be worth calling me if I missed a payment."

At the first opportunity, Bill moved all his accounts out of that bank, but that's another story. He turned to the local Haas distributor, Machining Time Savers in Anaheim, which financed the remaining $20,000 needed for the purchase. Action Mold never missed a payment and has since rewarded Machining Time Savers with three other equipment purchases, clearly a greater return than the interest on that first purchase.

Manufacturers and distributors of equipment are sometimes willing to help their customers finance purchases, especially the purchases of expensive machinery. Such capital assistance is often the difference between making the sale and walking away empty-handed. These financing deals are offered on more than manufacturing equipment. Suppliers of computers, software, mailing machinery, and high-speed printers, to name a few, will help finance a sale. The loan often comes at better interest rates than bank loans or credit cards. These sellers know that customers like Action Mold will tend to be loyal to a manufacturer or distributor that backs its sales pitch with capital financing. The lifetime value of such customers can be high if these companies grow and make repeated purchases from the same supplier, as did Action Mold, which has grown to multimillion-dollar annual sales and 25 employees.

Bill notes that this particular CNC machine was highly specialized for making one-of-a-kind molds, so Machining Time Savers would have few potential customers for it. "Many injection mold companies could use it if they took the time to figure it out. It had some quirks, but we were used to them and liked the machine."

Bill and Steve have made a steady habit of putting a third of their income back into Action Mold to buy equipment and stimulate growth. Such reinvestment of profits helps cut the company's income tax bill because of depreciation write-offs. Those tax savings reduce the actual cost of machinery while boosting the company's capability to take on more jobs in the future. In some cases, Action Mold has won contracts on the condition that it buys a specific piece of equipment or software, Bill adds. "One customer wanted us to have three-dimensional CAD [computer aided design] capabilities. We bought the CNC and software and they gave us the work, which more than paid for the equipment, and we could use it on other contracts."

SECTION C

GOVERNMENT PROGRAMS

■ ■ ■

Cities, states, and federal agencies have an interest in boosting the economy and number of jobs, which provide stable societies and better environments for residents and, let's face it, voters. Society in general also benefits from innovations and improved technologies, so some government entities seek ways to encourage research and development. Business owners who seek capital from the government are more likely to receive the grants, equity investments, or loans if they understand the obligation to create new technologies or more jobs.

77. COMMUNITY INVESTING PROGRAMS

A nationwide program encourages banks and investors
to invest 1 percent of their portfolios in businesses in
disadvantaged areas to strengthen local communities.

■ ■ ■

Wally Holmgren had been a dairy farmer in Southern California for years. When he retired to Myrtle Point, Oregon, in the mid-1980s, he initially bought a vineyard. But his son moved to the area and liked raising dairy cows more than growing grapes. The Holmgrens first converted their farm to a dairy and then sold it to buy a larger one. In 2000, they joined about six of their neighboring families in switching to an organic dairy in which no antibiotics are used and the cows graze in pastures instead of being fed in barns or feedlots.

"We wanted to get a bank loan to add a milking parlor and a new barn," Wally says. "I ran into a brick wall. Several banks we contacted weren't interested in farming. They didn't think we had a viable operation. They thought it was way too risky."

That's when Wally remembered ShoreBank Pacific had opened an office in the community of 2,500 and a representative had come around offering services.

"You can't imagine my surprise when I called and the representative in the local office came out in two hours, sat down, and worked out the loan terms," Wally says. "The interest rate is as good [as] or a little better than regular bank loans."

ShoreBank Pacific is one of many banks across America that has a commitment to community investing. The Social Investment Forum Foundation and Co-op America describe community investing as making loans and equity investments in businesses in economically disadvantaged areas in order to boost the local economy and provide jobs. The foundation asks participating banks and investors to commit 1 percent of their portfolios to community investing.

ShoreBank Pacific has a commitment to environmental businesses, such as "green" buildings, land trusts for open space, and the organic food industry, says spokesman Randell Leach. It has 6 percent of its loans totaling $3 million in this sector, including farms, shellfish and fish production, and food processors. The bank provides more than money. It helps its clients find ways to be sustainable and competitive against large corporations.

"It's a very different model for a bank. Our prime customers are those that align with our core values, which are to support the community and environment," Randell says. "Also sometimes we see an opportunity to change a community by focusing on another industry or making their product more than just a commodity, which can sell only at the lowest price."

For example, small dairy farms can't sell their milk for as low a price as large milk producers, so they need some way to differentiate their milk as a higher value product for which consumers are willing to pay more money. Milk from organic dairies has that differentiation.

With the help of ShoreBank Pacific's loan, Holmgren Dairy is success-ful and growing. It milks 220 cows a day, and Wally anticipates expanding to 350 cows. It sells its milk under the Organic Valley label through the Coulee Regional Organic Produce Pool, a co-op of more than 200 farms in 13 states.

"We have received a lot of support from the bank after the loan was made; they still visit," Wally says. "The longer we go, the better the rela-tionship."

78. GOVERNMENT ECONOMIC INCENTIVES

A growing business can often obtain loans and other
incentives from public agencies responsible for
developing local and state economies.

■ ■ ■

After a successful career as a tooling engineer, Tom Hoffman de-cided to start his own precision machining and tooling company, Summit Design and Manufacturing in Helena, Montana, in 1997. From three em-ployees plus Tom, Summit grew in five years to 50 full-time employees in Montana and 6 more employees in Marietta, Georgia. In 2002, the com-pany changed its name to Summit Aeronautics Group to emphasize its aerospace products and assemblies for companies worldwide. That growth was fueled by Summit's success at manufacturing tools and parts for the F-16 and other aircraft for customers including Boeing, Lockheed-Martin, and Bell Helicopter. Summit is a key component maker for the Air Force's F/A-22 Raptor, the most technologically advanced airplane built to date. And the potential for job growth made Summit eligible for various state and federal economic development incentives.

The University of Montana's Helena College of Technology received in 2004 a $100,000 federal grant for equipment and training for teachers who train workers how to manufacture composite materials for aircraft builders. Many of the students trained in the program work for Summit upon graduation. Summit also provides internships for machining and welding students from the college.

Tom's vision is to run a Montana-based and Montana-owned corporation dedicated to providing Montanans with quality jobs in the aerospace industry. The state of Montana hopes that Summit's success will attract other aerospace companies to the state.

Summit's ability to create jobs qualified the company for Montana's Value-Added Business Loan Program, which is funded from the state's permanent coal tax trust. Montana, like many states, has various loans, grants, and other incentive programs to attract and keep companies, especially if they bring jobs and spending to the state. Montana is unusual in funding some of its economic incentive programs with a tax on coal. Some of Montana's other programs help fund infrastructure or use coal tax revenues to buy a certificate of deposit equal to the loan made to a local business.

The Value-Added Business Loan Program is open only to companies whose manufacturing processes add value to materials or products. About 12, including Summit, have made use of these 15-year, fixed-interest-rate loans of $250,000 to $6.6 million. Summit qualified for the lowest interest rate of 2 percent for 5 years because it added at least 15 new jobs. The company used the loan to buy more machinery, which made it even more efficient and productive. Tom knows that having state-of-the-art equipment is vital to remaining competitive in the aerospace industry. Summit won a substantial contract with Boeing Military to machine the engine bay doors for the F-22 aircraft. Boeing said it evaluated every company competing for the contract, and Summit's equipment was the most accurate in the United States.

Summit's effective use of economic development incentives and training programs has earned the company a reputation for cost efficiency, competitive pricing, and a highly trained workforce.

79. SMALL BUSINESS INNOVATION RESEARCH GRANTS

The Small Business Innovation Research (SBIR) program
gives small technology companies access to research and
development dollars from large federal agencies.

■ ■ ■

Since 1988, materials scientist Rick Yoon has been custom designing technical components for clients at his company IJ Research Inc. in
Santa Ana, California. One of his specialties is heat dissipation; so when
the U.S. Navy sought proposals for new protective packaging for electronic components placed near hot jet engines, Rick jumped at the project.
He applied for and won an SBIR grant for $100,000 to explore the techni-
cal feasibility of his proposed solution to the Navy's problem. That contract was successful, so the Navy awarded IJ Research a second SBIR
grant of $750,000 to further develop the plan.

The SBIR program seeks to draw companies with fewer than 500 employees into federal funding for research and development. The reason is
simple: Most of the innovations in the twentieth century came from small
businesses. That trend is expected to continue in the twenty-first century;
so the 1982 Small Business Innovation Development Act requires the ten
federal agencies with the largest R&D budgets to award some of that
money to small business. Since that time, more than 41,000 small businesses have received more than $6.5 billion for research projects.

The money is awarded in phases. Phase I grants give a company up to
$100,000 to explore the feasibility of a proposed technological improve-
ment or new product. If successful, the company can seek up to $750,000
to further develop the project.

However, it's tough to win an SBIR contract. Only about 1 in every 20
applicants receives a Phase I contract and only companies with a Phase I
contract can apply for Phase II grants. In 2002, the ten agencies awarded
4,138 Phase I contracts and 1,595 Phase II contracts.

Not only that, not every company is eligible. The firm must be a privately owned, for-profit entity with fewer than 500 employees. And the
owner must be a U.S. citizen.

Since winning the first two Navy SBIR contracts, Rick has won others from the Navy for electronic controls for ships' cannons and from the Army for methods to deflect heat inside tanks and to build a more efficient radiator for military vehicles.

"We write 20 proposals for every contract we win," Rick says. "I've always had competition for the work. Many times I get a good feeling that I will get the contract, and then I don't win."

He is continually looking for requests for SBIR proposals. The government used to publish a booklet of opportunities, but now everything is on the Internet. "I type DOD [Department of Defense, which awards half the SBIR contracts] and SBIR in the search engines and get a lot," he says. "We used to file thick applications by mail, but now you must apply electronically."

The other federal agencies that participate in the SBIR program are the Department of Agriculture (USDA), Department of Commerce (DOC), Department of Education (ED), Department of Energy (DOE), Department of Health and Human Services (HHS), Department of Transportation (DOT), Environmental Protection Agency (EPA), National Aeronautics and Space Administration (NASA), and National Science Foundation (NSF).

Rick is careful not to allow SBIR contracts to dominate his company. They represent, at most, 15 percent of revenues. He has five other divisions, which give IJ Research diversity. That keeps the company strong even when one area weakens, as the telecommunications industry did a few years ago.

In addition to intense competition, the SBIR program is time-consuming. "Many people don't apply for SBIR contracts because it takes enormous effort and time," Rick says. "It's a lot of paperwork. I have to work on it day and night."

80. STATE JOB TRAINING GRANTS

Companies that offer job-related instruction to employees may
be eligible for grants from the state to cover their costs.

■ ■ ■

When Anita Burns became the first human resources director at
Machine Solutions Inc. in Flagstaff, Arizona, the company gave her a to-
do list that included seeking grant money. One possibility was the Arizona
job training grant program. Employers pay a tax of up to $7 per employee
into a fund that finances job-specific training within companies. Most
states coordinate job training programs funded by the federal government,
which spends about $12 billion annually on such training. And almost half
the states have employment placement and job training programs financed
by taxes on employers, as Arizona does, according to the federal Government Accountability Office in 2004. Arizona's employer tax raises more
than $12 million a year for training grants. A fourth of the money is set
aside for small businesses and a fourth for rural areas.

However, Anita thought Machine Solutions might not qualify for a
grant because the company never had any formal orientation program. But
Arizona's program actually favors companies that have no training programs because it requires companies to use the grant money to augment,
not replace, existing spending on employee training.

Each state's job training grant programs have different requirements.
Arizona demands that participating companies pay a specified wage or
higher, which varies in different locations throughout the state. A grant-
winning firm must also pay 25 percent of the training costs for new employees and 50 percent of training for its existing workforce. The purpose
of the state's program is to meet company needs for an educated and
trained workforce, to help create new jobs, and to boost workers' skills and
wages. For qualifying companies, such programs provide useful capital,
preserve assets for other needs, and build a better workforce. However,
companies that win such grants must plan their cash flow because some
states do not release the money until after the training is complete.

With the help of the Greater Flagstaff Economic Council, Machine Solutions applied for and received $160,608 in 2004 for various training efforts. The company is ideal for the program's intention. It manufactures custom equipment, such as catheter testing machines, mainly for medical companies worldwide, so its skilled jobs help build the state's technology base. After starting in a garage in 2000, Machine Solutions grew to 45 employees by mid-2004 and planned to add another 30 workers by the end of the year, says cofounder Dan Kasprzyk.

"We have been very successful growing the company without help; but it's nice to have a grant for job training," he says.

The application process was fairly simple, Anita says. The state asked for such information as financials, plans for growth, costs to put a new hire into a job, and what the training needs were. The Greater Flagstaff Economic Council reviewed the draft and helped hone the final submission, she adds.

The Arizona Department of Commerce announced the award in August 2004 and the training began for newly hired workers about a month later. Some states also require pay raises and guaranteed jobs for a period of time for employees going through state-funded training. Arizona does not have such a retention requirement on the company nor does the state lock the workers in to their current jobs for a specified period after training.

SECTION D

GET CREATIVE

■ ■ ■

Commitment to business ownership spurs imaginative thinking when it comes to finding capital to maintain or grow a company or provide equipment or niceties the owner might otherwise not be able to afford. Look at company resources. Seek out contests. Leverage spending to provide company needs at lower or no cost. Put talents and resources on the line to meet the company's financial needs. That's how entrepreneurs think.

81.

SELL PART
OF YOUR RIGHTS

When developing a new product, you can raise capital by
selling part ownership in the concept to outside investors.

■ ■ ■

After owning a couple of companies in tool making and auto resto-
ration, Eliot Geeting started developing his own inventions full-time in
1986. Sometimes his firm, Eliot James Enterprises in Dana Point, California, would take a product from idea to market. But most of the time, Eliot
looked for other companies to license his products at the prototype stage.
Even so, product development requires creativity in obtaining the capital
needed to get a product to market and then to market it to profitability.

Such was the case with the BugStik, Eliot's invention for either catch-
ing or killing household bugs without touching the critters. The BugStik
looks like a sink scrubber on a pole. It can capture a spider or insect, transport it outside and eject it into the garden. Or it can kill it and dispose it
into the trash. Eliot applied for a provisional patent on the BugStik and
built a prototype to create a promotional "sell sheet" and demonstrate the
product's effectiveness in order to persuade product manufacturers to license it.

"Before I got the deal closed, I gave 5 percent interest in the product
to one investor in exchange for his Corvette, which was worth approximately $25,000," Eliot says. "I sold the car and used the proceeds for op-
erating my business, and later to invest in inventory after I had to cancel
the licensing deal as a result of the licensee not meeting the terms of the
licensing agreement."

Eliot believes that an entrepreneur must never be so attached to a product or idea that he won't give up a portion of it in exchange for working
capital. His own investment in the BugStik was just a couple of hundred
dollars. It has grossed more than $1 million in sales. The tricky part is es-
tablishing the future value of a product. Eliot has given up as much as 60
percent of a product concept to bring an investor in at an early stage. The
more work Eliot does in patenting, building, and marketing a product, the
less ownership he sells. With the BugStik, ultimately, the investor had to

agree that the device was likely to be so successful that 5 percent owner-ship of it was worth more than $25,000. On the other hand, Eliot had to be flexible enough to accept a Corvette in payment on the belief that he could sell it for the $25,000 he needed to move the BugStik toward licensing and onto store shelves. Those types of creative capital commitments are plen-tiful in the product development arena.

For another product, Eliot accepted $50,000 in payments over several years from a licensee that could fully exploit the product's potential but didn't want to be cash poor by paying the entire fee up front.

"I secured the payments with a note and first trust deed on a piece of commercial property the company owned," Eliot says. "They wanted to get the deal done without having to dip into operating capital and without having to go to the bank. So I figured the first trust deed on a piece of prop-erty that was worth $1.4 million was as good as cash. The deal gave us all what we needed."

82. CONTEST WINNINGS

Business contests can provide capital for strategic
expansions or improvements.

■ ■ ■

Thomas Testa and James Perry, partners in Alliance Portfolio, a pri-vate commercial real estate lender in Newport Beach, California, decided in early 2004 to delay a planned purchase of new computer servers and software in order to afford other business priorities. Then Orlando Flores, IT director for the 12-employee firm, came across an announcement for Microsoft's Technology Makeover Contest. Entry was simple. Write 500 words about why your company deserves $75,000 in technology and services.

"I entered it figuring, at worst, I'd get a bunch of brochures and sales calls," Orlando says.

In his essay, Orlando explained Alliance Portfolio's desire to connect databases in separate offices without using the Internet because of security concerns. Alliance had worked for two years with two different consultants searching for an affordable solution. A glitch wiped out Orlando's original essay from Microsoft's entry Web site, so he reconstructed his information in a series of follow-up e-mails.

From 7,000 entries, Alliance Portfolio won one of two national prizes.

Business owners shouldn't depend on contests to keep their companies solvent, but prize money or equipment can achieve strategic improvements and preserve cash flow for other purposes.

"A month before the contest we had decided to delay [the project]," Tom says. "The contest suddenly made it possible."

The Internet makes the search for such contests much easier than it used to be. Orlando was searching Web sites for software the company needed when he found Microsoft's competition. Technology companies have been especially fond of contests because product prizes can be quite inexpensive for them and popular with their targeted markets. But don't overlook targeted industry magazines for news items and ads about contests tailor-made for your business. Don't ignore direct mail announcements either.

In Alliance Portfolio's win, Microsoft didn't merely write a check. The software giant wanted to demonstrate its capabilities for complex office technology for companies with fewer than 50 employees. In judging the contest, Microsoft sought smaller businesses with common issues and technology concerns, such as cost, redundancies, and security. Alliance Portfolio provided a good example of how technology could improve work flow, productivity, and in-house communications. The hard-money lender both originates mortgages in one office and services them in the other. Because the two offices' databases weren't connected, employees spent hours reentering information. A solution would yield huge productivity gains.

Microsoft partners sat down with Alliance Portfolio executives to create a comprehensive plan for infrastructure, services, hardware, and software to achieve the company's productivity goals. In fact, one of the stumbling blocks for small businesses trying to capitalize on technology efficiencies is their lack of infrastructure to make the most effective use of equipment and software. Alliance Portfolio had already done about half the work, which made the $75,000 stretch even further.

"I think they were surprised at our level of sophistication," Tom says, adding that the preparation probably contributed to Alliance Portfolio winning the contest.

Along with the analysis and infrastructure plan, Alliance Portfolio received an MS Small Business Server 2003, notebook personal computers, two wireless tablet personal computers, a specialized database, and business contact software.

"In just the data entry process alone, we expect to see significant improvement," Tom says. "Companywide we're looking at 25 percent to 40 percent time savings."

The efficiencies enabled Alliance Portfolio to expand quickly, doubling its staff within the year following the contest win.

83. DEATH-DEFYING ACTS

Entrepreneurs committed to making their ventures
succeed must sometimes go to great lengths to
acquire the capital needed to keep going.

■ ■ ■

Jim McCafferty started teaching himself magic tricks when he was nine years old. He poured over how-to books and performed a lot of horrible shows until he was good enough that audiences didn't get up and walk out. Eventually he started winning school talent shows and by the time he was in high school, Jim was making more money performing magic than his teachers earned instructing students. He even won a world magic competition in Las Vegas.

Jim started hiring people for his business, JMP Creative in Santa Ana, California, and eventually segued from entertaining performances to marketing his firm's creative abilities. JMP Creative is neither a toy manufacturer nor advertising agency. Its creativity consultants help ad agencies develop imaginative marketing campaigns, toy companies invent new products, and movie studios enhance their film magic.

However, more than once during JMP Creative's infancy, payday came before clients' checks. "When cash got low, I had to go figure out how to get enough money to keep the company going," Jim remembers. "One thing I knew I could do that would raise enough money fast enough to meet payroll was perform death-defying acts. As an entrepreneur you say, 'OK, I'll go risk my life to save the company.'"

Among his bag of magic tricks were Houdini-like escapes from water tanks and cages hanging by a burning rope.

One time, Jim contacted a large group in Northern California about providing the entertainment for a charity fundraising event. He told the group to build any type of container it wanted, lock him inside, and he would escape or die trying. "These death-defying performances can bring $20,000 to $50,000 and up. No one pays you that much unless someone might die," he says. "Danger sells a lot of tickets."

Jim knows how to build multiple safeguards into his escape stunts, but they're still dangerous, and things can go wrong.

For the Northern California charity event to be held on Halloween night in a museum, a welder built a glass tank for an underwater escape attempt. Radio ads promoted the stunt as the "underwater walls of death." The day of the event, Jim had to change his escape strategy because the tank had been modified from Jim's original plans.

"I used to make my living doing this and have had to change strategy during the escape when things aren't working," Jim says. "Those performances prepared me for entrepreneurship, because in both you can't panic. You have to stop, change your plan quickly before you run out of air or money."

Halloween night, a fire truck came to fill the tank. The water was extremely cold and murky, which Jim hadn't expected. Still, he managed to escape the "walls of death" and to meet November payroll.

Jim scheduled these events more than once to pull JMP Creative through its start-up phase, but today he pulls millions of dollars in revenue from clients without the death-defying showmanship.

"You never feel like your staff appreciates what you do to cover payroll when you have to risk death," Jim laughs. "It never failed. Someone always asked for a raise after the really dangerous escapes."

84.

FRIENDS OF
THE LIBRARY

Small business owners become creative when they look for
sources of capital to keep a company stable during slow times.

■ ■ ■

Jane Bayer sells facts. Her Lake Forest, California, business consulting company, Factfinders, does research mostly for law firms. Her work involves everything from identifying expert witnesses who support her client's position in a legal proceeding to gathering information about an opponent's position. She first started Factfinders while living in Germany in 1992. Because the advent of the Internet has made so much information available, Jane has also trained others in the tricks and tips of doing their own research. They often find easily uncovered facts themselves but must return to Jane for more advanced work.

Although the need for information and research training continues to grow, business—and therefore cash flow—is sometimes slow. More than once, Jane has attended book sales for her local Friends of the Library group, buying for pennies reference books, year-old association directories, database volumes, and other professional publications that sell for hundreds of dollars when new.

"I can turn around and resell many of them for $150 or more," Jane says. "For the individual businessperson, the cost of such volumes is prohibitive so they visit the local library to look something up. If they can have it in their office, it's a time saver."

And the book sales carry Factfinders through lean times. Her customers are often fellow researchers in the Association of Independent Professionals, many of whom have left corporate jobs like Jane did to run home-based businesses. An engineer by training, Jane got fed up with the extreme highs and lows of the aerospace industry. Yet she still copes with such capital fluctuations in Factfinders. "Selling books helped the business survive in 1998 when we moved back to the United States," she says.

Millions of Americans run one-person home businesses whose capital needs are not exorbitant. They find many creative ways to fill in the funding gaps. In other chapters of this book, business owners have sold personal possessions on eBay, traded valuable collections for cash, turned volatile stocks for quick gains, and entered contests to help finance the start or continuing operation of their ventures. Business ownership brings out creativity and persistence that many people never realize they have until they need to save their "baby," the business.

"I always wanted to run my own shop," Jane says. "When I started in 1992 I was just hearing tidbits about the Internet. I thought it was going to take off, and people would be overwhelmed with too much information. They would need experts to sift out the useful from the meaningless.

"It took lots of years to grow the business and become an expert myself," Jane says. "Many of my clients are attorneys who don't have time to do this research. Another group of clients are entrepreneurs who have a great idea and don't know how to move it into a business plan. I don't write the plan for them, but I do all the industry demographics and customer profiles that go into the plan. I also identify venture capitalists who might fund their idea."

85. BARTER

Trading your goods and services for those of another
company that your business needs can save
capital and preserve cash flow.

■ ■ ■

Ann Crane had managed the catering side of Meyerhof's Cuisine M in Irvine, California, for 12 years when the owner died in 1995. The company had several divisions, including food manufacturing for restaurants. Ann offered to buy the catering service in 1996, later changing the name to Meyerhof's Fine Catering. Some of the essential equipment remained with the other company, so Ann needed to replace it.

She acquired a large amount of used equipment from an auction house, but instead of paying in cash, she swapped the sandwiches served during the auction for a six-burner stove, double-stacked oven, stainless steel tables, shelving, and more.

Entrepreneurs have been bartering goods and services since ancient times. In North America approximately 200,000 businesses bartered more than $2 billion worth of products and activities in 2004, according to the National Association of Trade Exchanges. The practice is quite legal as long as the parties pay taxes on the products they receive in trade just as they would with cash revenues. Companies of all sizes use barter to attract new customers, unload excess inventory without angering regular customers, and preserve cash, as Ann did.

"It's important to spell out exactly what you are bartering and how you are pricing the goods or services," Ann says. "I make it clear I am valuing my food at the price I would charge at retail."

Setting the appropriate price is perhaps the toughest part of bartering. Inexperienced barterers tend to give up too much for too little in return. Novices also tend to get caught up in obtaining stuff seemingly for free and trade for items they don't need or wouldn't buy with cash. Companies that barter regularly need to set a limit, such as using barter for no more than 5 percent of revenues each month and compiling a needs list before going bartering.

A company cannot survive on bartering. It must have cash for utilities, payroll, taxes, and interest on debt. Companies with high fixed costs, such as hotels and restaurants, are attracted to regular bartering through one of the 500 organized exchange clubs throughout North America. A hotel has to pay its employees and electricity bill whether its rooms are rented or not. An empty room might represent $100 in lost revenue each night. If it can trade a one-night stay for $100 worth of printing, the hotel gets something it needs.

Exchange clubs charge a fee but offer a wider choice of goods and services. The florist can provide flowers to a hotel, which trades a room to an electrician who does work for a plumber who unclogs the florist's sinks. Direct barter depends on two businesses wanting exactly what the other has to offer.

Ann doesn't use bartering on a regular basis for Meyerhof's Fine Catering, but has exchanged her services and food for public relations services and interior design services. "We sit down ahead of time and say, 'This is what I would charge you for my services,' balance the two, and then swap," she says.

86. CASH FLOW FROM SURPLUS SPACE

A business with excess office or warehouse space can
bring in additional capital through a sublease.

■ ■ ■

Growing businesses sometimes make a mistake leasing offices, stores, or warehouses sufficient for their current needs and face a space squeeze within a year or two. A better strategy is to lease or buy a building based on calculations of needs to match future growth, says Jay Furry, for many years a sales executive with Century Electric Motors in St. Louis, Missouri.

In the late 1980s, Jay's Northern California distributor wanted to move out of San Francisco, which had high taxes and onerous laws affecting small businesses. In nearby Pleasanton, two adjacent units with twice the square footage previously used for distribution, storage, and repair were available at enticingly low rent if the distributor signed a ten-year lease.

"Unfortunately, current sales didn't support that rent, especially because this was a new market for us," Jay says.

Signing long-term leases for more than a business can afford could be a recipe for cash flow disaster. But this arrangement turned out well because of creativity and flexibility.

Once all the repair tools, equipment, and electric motor inventory were moved into the new headquarters, there was significant empty space, Jay says. Good for future growth, but a waste in the interim.

"So I suggested subleasing the extra space," Jay says. "Get the word around to other businesses in the area."

A nearby carpet business had a space crunch with carpet rolls piled to the rafters and practically pouring out the door. That owner was interested in getting some extra space nearby and was willing to pay a higher rate than the distributor was paying.

"During my travels I have noticed that a lot of small-business owners rent out space when they have extra room in their warehouses or repair facilities," Jay says.

The original lease must allow subleasing of space under reasonable conditions. Some landlords insist on the right to veto sublease deals, but tenants should fight hard to keep this clause as flexible as possible, even if subleasing is the furthest thing from their minds. In an economic downturn, a business might have to make drastic cutbacks. The ability to sublease unused space can be the difference between survival and bankruptcy.

"Sometimes this really works well for both small companies," Jay says. "I know of one instance where a motor repair company subleased to an electrical contractor, which removed and replaced large motors that needed maintenance or repairs. In return, the electrical contractor brought all other motor repairs to the motor repair company. That arrangement lasted for about eight or nine years and allowed both companies to grow rapidly."

In the case of Century's electric motor distributor, the carpet company paid $600 a month for space on a month-to-month agreement. That extra cash saved the distributor during a transition period and preserved the adjacent space for future growth.

"This arrangement lasted for about three years," Jay says. "Our distribution facility had use of 75 percent of the total space, and the carpet guy paid for a third of the monthly lease. When the carpet company relocated to larger quarters, we had grown enough to need all the space."

87. MAXIMIZE FREQUENT FLIER MILES

Bonuses offered with credit cards can preserve
precious cash for required expenditures.

■ ■ ■

Cheryl Moore has always been a saver. "I enjoy saving money like other people enjoy spending it," she says. In the consumer world this attitude translates into shopping the ads for discounts, coupon clipping, and eating dinner before 5:00 PM to take advantage of restaurants' early-bird specials. In the business world, this philosophy means getting someone else to pay for essentials.

Cheryl owns Something Moore, a women's clothing and accessories store in Laguna Niguel, California. She pays for business expenses and for inventory with a credit card that awards frequent flier miles. And then she uses those frequent flier miles for airline tickets to take buying trips for her store.

"Years ago manufacturers would offer terms like 30 days net [to pay invoices]," Cheryl says. "Now more and more of them want their money right away. Using a credit card allows me to do that, and I still get something of value out of it."

She flies to New York three times a year, to Dallas twice a year, and occasionally to Atlanta for shows of the latest merchandise, a necessity for a women's clothing store. She estimates that frequent flier miles save her $1,200 to $1,300 in airline tickets annually. For an independent retailer, such savings are vital.

"In my business, I buy so much—$10,000 a month—that I can get a free ticket every four or five months," Cheryl says. "I don't always use my frequent flier miles for my flights. Sometimes the airlines offer such low fares that I will go ahead and take advantage of that bargain. I don't like to use 20,000 frequent flier points for a low-price ticket. I use them for the more expensive flights, so that I get more out of the transaction."

Rules for cashing in frequent flier miles typically require a reservation at least a month before traveling, but that's no problem for Cheryl because the show dates are announced far in advance.

Cheryl made a deliberate decision to obtain and use a credit card that awarded frequent flier miles. When the one she was using stopped this particular benefit, Cheryl looked for another. She also chose a credit card issued by a major bank, rather than a card from one airline, so that she could use her frequent flier miles with any carrier, which increased the flexibility of her schedule and choice of airport, which is important in a metropolitan area like Southern California, which has more than six airports.

Cheryl only used her credit cards for inventory at her store, but she has business friends who put every company expense, even their taxes, on the credit card that awards frequent flier miles. Cheryl thinks that's a bad idea because government taxing agencies charge a fee.

Although Cheryl buys on credit from many different suppliers, she is cautious about giving her credit card number out, especially at trade shows. "The [manufacturers'] reps carry all their orders in their luggage. If that gets stolen, so does my credit card number, and identity theft is always a concern," she explains. "If I'm at a show and they take credit cards, I tell them to call me when they're ready to ship and I give them the number at that time." Her suppliers are satisfied with that arrangement and Cheryl gets both identity protection and bonus miles from the purchases.

88.   DISCOUNTS

A business may actually stimulate cash flow or larger
sales by offering customers a discount. But strings
should be attached to avoid losses.

■ ■ ■

College mathematics professor Steve Alemansour has tutored elementary, high school, and college students since 1989 through his company, Academy of Tutoring Professionals in Lake Forest, California. The business, while lucrative, is also highly seasonal. Steve typically charges $40, $45, or $50 an hour depending on the difficulty of the subject being tutored. Academy of Tutoring Professionals has more work than the staff of experts can handle after midterm grades come out and before final exams. But during the summer and early in the new term, revenues slow significantly.

"If we can presell our tutoring services, it helps fill in a little during the slow months," Steve says. "Typically, during August and into the early fall we offer a 5 percent or 10 percent discount for purchasing tutoring hours in advance. They must pay by a certain date."

That discount not only serves to bring in cash during a lean period of the year but students and parents often buy more hours of service than they would if they bought them week to week, Steve says. Clients are especially willing to buy additional hours at a discount if the subject is a difficult one, such as physics, in which the student is likely to need help throughout the term.

"We offer the discount to existing clients through a mailer at the end of the summer," Steve says. "We also offer it to people who call after seeing our Yellow Pages ad. Some students and parents will buy 30 or 50 hours of tutoring for the coming semester and then come back and buy more right before the deadline for taking advantage of the discount."

Many seasonal businesses use discounts to level the hills and valleys of revenue throughout the year, but discounts serve other capital purposes as well. Many companies use discounts to reward regular customers, which is likely to encourage them to remain loyal and to spend more, thereby increasing their lifetime value to the company. Companies boost cash flow by giving discounts for early payment or cash on delivery. They also may increase revenues by giving discounts for large-volume purchases. Discounts for longer term contracts can stabilize a company's long-term financial situation, which helps forecasting and planning. During bad economic times, a discount can be a better way to encourage sales than cutting prices outright because raising prices later is problematic, driving a certain percentage of customers away.

Each of these uses of discounts can help a company's capital position. However, the company must carefully track its revenues and profits to avoid charging less for its products or services than those items cost to provide. Also, a business that advertises "interest-free credit" must not offer a discount for cash. It is false advertising to give a discount for immediate payment because it implies that the full price includes a dollar amount for interest.

"I've been using discounts for three years; I don't know of a down side," Steve says. "It makes sense. My customers put their purchase on a credit card so they earn extra mileage or other bonuses; they get services for less money, and my cash flow improves during those slow months."

89. SPONSORSHIPS

If you can attract a large customer base, product and service companies will step up with product and cash sponsorships that multiply your available capital.

■ ■ ■

Brothers Sonny and Quang Nguyen launched National Gaming Association in Garden Grove, California, in 2002 to capitalize on the online video game industry that has 60 million players in the United States alone and is growing exponentially. The industry is even bigger in other nations, such as Korea, which features events on prime time television.

The online company, NGAsports.com, seeks to standardize the electronic games and make competition more professional by organizing competitive leagues and tournaments, keeping statistics on registered players, and providing a source of all news about the online video game industry.

"NGAsports.com was made especially with the gamer in mind," says Quang, chief executive of National Gaming Association. "Our site captures what it means to be a gamer and what it means to be part of the gaming culture."

NGAsports.com's national finals to select U.S. representatives to the 2004 Electronic Sports World Cup in France attracted more than 100,000 online viewers and several hundred spectators to the Nguyens' ICE Internet Café, physical site of the tournament. The costs of the event were largely borne by sponsorships from makers of video games, equipment, and food eager to get their names and products in front of a large, targeted audience.

These highly coveted and lucrative sponsorships aren't easy to obtain, says Sonny, NGAsports.com president. To fork over cash, a company usually wants to be a tournament's title sponsor. NVIDIA Corp., a Santa Clara, California company specializing in visual technology for computers, was the worldwide sponsor of the Electronic Sports Cup in 2004. The company worked with all the firms putting on national finals, including NGAsports .com.

But NGAsports.com worked for two years to get that recognition, Sonny says. "It's a gradual process. If you're putting on an event, the most important thing is for sponsors to trust you and feel comfortable working with your company."

The first event is the toughest for attracting sponsorships, he says, because a company has no track record. He and Quang did a lot of cold calling to potential sponsors. They attended game development conferences, trade shows, and expos, getting their company name and their own presence in front of potential sponsors.

"We started out slowly because they needed to know who we are and what our company is capable of doing," Sonny says. "All the sponsors know each other; the marketing directors talk to each other about companies like ours. Once you're in the loop, it's easier to get sponsors."

Each Internet video gaming competition had to attract great players, large audiences, and enthusiasm among chat rooms and blogs that freely comment on the industry. As NGAsports.com generated more coverage and conversation, it received attention and then products from sponsoring companies.

"They will give products for us for prizes and to give to the competitors to see what benefits they receive, what their return on investment is," Sonny says. "If we attract a lot of players or spectators, there's a benefit to the sponsors."

At the 2004 national finals, video games, equipment, mouse pads, T-shirts, and more from sponsors were stacked eye-high around the venue. Sponsor banners hung from the rafters. Several game makers set up computers where spectators could test the games themselves. Tables piled high with food for players and spectators had placards with sponsors' names.

But that level of sponsorship was built on putting on successful events and constantly contacting product companies to show off a growing portfolio of events and online traffic to NGAsports.com.

90. THE STOCK MARKET

Equity ownership in public companies can increase
in value to provide capital for a private firm.

■ ■ ■

Kim Jorgenson had been a successful event planner for many years when she bought a bakery and converted the 1,200-square-foot facility into Plums Café & Catering in Costa Mesa, California, in 1990. The restaurant was still building its clientele when a recession hit. Kim's established event planning company lost a great deal of business as companies and individuals stopped holding lavish parties. Soon, Kim's finances were so low that she wondered how she would pay the monthly rent for Plums Café.

"I didn't come from money," Kim says, "so I had to do everything myself. I couldn't turn to family to get cash for the rent."

Kim occasionally dabbled in the stock market, more for fun than profit. On the suggestion of a friend, she bought stock in a company that pioneered in bottled mineral water. Its stock was volatile, to say the least.

"My friend thought I was crazy; I was down to the last bit of money in my checking account," Kim says. "I said if I don't do this, I won't have my rent money anyway."

Fortunately for Kim, she bought low, the stock spiked, and she sold the stock to make the $1,500 she needed for the rent.

To anyone who has never owned a business, it sounds risky and impetuous. But many business owners take such steps multiple times during their entrepreneurial lives to save their businesses. The only difference between Kim and Donald Trump's recapitalization of his crumbling real estate empire is the number of zeros behind the dollar sign.

The stock market has been a source of start-up, growth, and survival capital for many more companies than those listed on the various stock exchanges. The enormous run-up in stocks during the late 1990s created instant wealth that many people cashed in to provide capital for their own companies. The Dow Jones Industrial Average rose from under 4,000 in 1995 to an all-time high of 11,722.98 on Jan. 14, 2000. But at less spectacular times, business owners like Kim have found their stock earnings to be company-saving assets. Investment experts wouldn't recommend some of the buys and sells that have propelled entrepreneurial ventures, but the owners aren't trying to get rich on their stock choices; they want to earn their fortunes in private businesses of their own.

Plums Café, for example, grew from its 1,200-square-foot shop to a 4,100-square-foot upscale bistro by 1999, thanks to the fact that Kim made a quick stock sale six years earlier. She continued to run the catering business from the same facility.

"I have continued to buy stock," she says. "It's fun. It's a hobby, a lot like gambling in Las Vegas. I'm really conservative with my business money. I don't use it to buy stock. The only money I put into the stock market these days is money I can afford to lose."

Once, during the late 1990s boom, Kim got online and bought some stock, leaving a sell order if the stock's price rose above a certain dollar amount. She went to the bathroom and when she came back, the sell order had been executed. She made $10,000 on the transaction.

"But I was not desperate for the money; it was more like playing," Kim says. "The $1,500 I made [in the mineral water company] meant more to me than the $10,000 or any other stock trade I have made since then because I was tapped out. I would have lost my business without it."

As it is, she still owns a thriving restaurant and catering business.

SECTION **E**

OTHER PEOPLE'S MONEY

■ ■ ■

Once a business model has been proven, an entrepreneur can often find people with money who are willing to invest in order to participate in the growth and profits. Just as loans are more readily available, so is equity capital. This may take the form of an individual who will buy a franchise to capitalize on the original success, companies that want to partner, professional investors who seek management roles as well as profits, and venture capitalists who want high-growth returns on investment.

91. FRANCHISING

A profitable, systematic business can expand without
borrowing or giving up equity by selling franchises.

■ ■ ■

Larry Green and Doug Lueck started Systems Paving Inc. in Newport Beach, California, in 1992 to build patios and driveways with interlocking stones, a method that had been more popular in Europe than the United States. The growth potential in this country was enormous. But Larry and Doug wanted to grow slowly and methodically, establishing the right systems, creating employee training, and developing the measurement tools that would make Systems Paving a long-lasting company. Even so, annual sales growth has been in the double digits from the beginning.

After nine years, Systems Paving had the systems in place to take the next expansion step: franchising.

Franchising sells a brand and system for doing business that can allow a company to grow rapidly with little of its own capital without giving up control of the business. Even though the best known franchises are fast-food restaurants like McDonald's, this method of business ownership is quite diversified. More than 2,300 companies in 75 different industries sell franchises in North America. Those companies have 768,000 franchises with combined annual revenues of $625 billion.

Some entrepreneurs start companies with the intent to franchise and start selling units in a year or less. Systems Paving wanted to prove first that the company's system could be duplicated. So it opened several corporate-owned satellite offices first.

"We gave managers of those offices a lot of autonomy and when we looked at the structure and operation down the road, they looked a lot like franchises," Larry says.

For these satellite offices, and later for franchisees, the company created Systems Paving University to train sales personnel and later field supervisors and construction managers. The company also created a sophisticated direct mail campaign model that could be duplicated in any geographic market. It developed proprietary software to track each job and to give homeowners a simulated three-dimensional look at their own property with paved patios and driveways. Once Systems Paving started selling franchises, it offered these corporate systems, training, and proprietary software as part of the franchise package if franchisees wanted them.

Systems Paving designates geographic territories for its franchisees. The size of the territory is based on the number of single-family homes with the target family income in the area. Some franchisors allow their franchisees to compete with each other in one market. Systems Paving, like most franchisors, charges a royalty on gross sales and stipulates that a certain percentage of sales must be spent on local advertising. Some franchisors charge an advertising fee and set up and run the promotional programs.

This income is sizable, but only about 10 percent of Systems Paving's annual revenue. "You don't want to have to sell franchises to survive," Larry says. "We don't need the money from franchising to survive, so we don't have to grow at the speed of light."

The significant part of franchising for Systems Paving is the growth it permits without huge capital expenditures by the corporate parent. Systems Paving still isn't seeking huge growth. It is awarding four to six franchises a year. A franchisor must provide support for its franchisees, so a company must not grow faster than its ability to give that support, Larry says.

Franchising has a benefit beyond money, he adds. "Franchising has made us even better. It brings people with a pride of ownership that's better than just being an employee. They don't work until the shift is over; they work 'til the job is done. When you bring in good people, it helps your own operation too."

92. LICENSING

Licensing your technology can give an infusion of
capital and build confidence in new technology in
order to increase future sales.

■ ■ ■

When Ken Virgin, Robert Ripley, and Jon Titel started iPayables in Lake Forest, California, in 1999, Internet technology was booming. The common expectation was to win full funding from venture capitalists within six months, a public offering within another year, and then be financially set for life.

Then the dot-com boom went bust.

The trio was creating Internet invoicing for large companies that would save money, track payments, and eliminate time-consuming data entry. Typically, Fortune 1,000 corporations are reluctant to adopt new technology, instead waiting for a solution from a brand-name company or testimonials from happy customers who have pioneered the use of the product.

iPayables survived only because its best customer helped engineer a licensing agreement that made iPayables invoicing solution, called Invoice-Works, a standard for the airline industry.

iPayables started with a direct sales force like so many of the Internet application providers in the late 1990s. But the sales cycle was extremely long for the nation's largest corporations. During iPayables's early years, it was trying to persuade cautious corporate buyers that the company was stable and could survive while other dot-com companies were filing bankruptcies daily.

Finally, American Airlines adopted InvoiceWorks because the airline's electronic bill-paying system could not be used for 17 percent of its invoices. iPayables's system quickly and simply converted those accounts to Internet invoicing. Other companies, including some airlines, were impressed with the system but refused to part with their cash to a relatively inexperienced company.

"It was clear by the end of 2002 we weren't going to burst through to profitability by the direct sales model," Ken says. He eliminated iPayables's sales force and started looking for partnerships.

American Airlines went to bat for iPayables, encouraging the International Air Transport Association (IATA) to license InvoiceWorks for all its airline members.

"Trade associations' main goal is to provide benefits to their members," Ken says. "If they could provide Internet invoicing, they would get what they wanted, which was the appreciation of their members."

IATA representatives weren't convinced that iPayables's system was the best, so they asked other airlines what systems they liked.

"All the other airlines knew who we were and liked what we were doing," Ken says. "So IATA asked, 'All we have to do is put our name on it and you'll buy it?' The other airlines said yes."

But IATA is a nonprofit association and doesn't have the resources to license products or services directly, so its officials started taking iPayables to third parties to discuss doing the licensing deal. BearingPoint Inc., a large consulting and systems integration firm in McLean, Virginia, signed a six-year licensing agreement with iPayables in 2003 for exclusive rights to provide iPayables's technology to the airline industry.

That deal put iPayables on profitable ground and ensured its long-term survival, even though the firm had to give up much of the long-term profit potential in that agreement in order to make the deal work. As Ken negotiates other licensing agreements, he has the financial stability to insist on terms more favorable to iPayables.

"Going from industry to industry is a great strategy, but it's not that easy to take over an entire industry," Ken explains. "Many associations would rather their members were using [technology] first and then they would put their name on it. Even with IATA, we were up against five other potential solutions. We won because all the airlines knew us and wanted us.

"We eventually will have a direct sales force, but I'm glad we did not go the venture capital route," Ken adds. "Because we were forced to go a different direction, we are in a much better financial position today."

93. SELL PART OWNERSHIP IN THE BUSINESS

If you lack sufficient capital to grow your company properly,
consider selling a portion of the business to the right buyer
in an arrangement that benefits all parties.

■ ■ ■

In 2001, Press Thornton and Mike Pierce quit their jobs to start ECHO LLC in Dothan, Alabama, to help large and mid-sized companies be more efficient in buying and distributing supplies. They focused on the retail, health care, heavy industrial, freight, and telecommunications industries.

But the partners didn't have enough capital to execute their plan fully and properly, so they took their business plan to friends Joe Malugen and Harrison Parrish, founders of Movie Gallery, also based in Dothan, a publicly traded movie video specialty retail chain with more than 2,000 stores.

"They liked the idea, gave us the capital to acquire a third of our company and gave us all their [procurement] business," Press says.

The investment wasn't just to help out a friend. ECHO, through its XPress Source subsidiary, allows client companies to outsource their procurement services, which saves more than 20 percent of buying costs for most clients and satisfies shareholder concerns about integrity in the buying process. Movie Gallery, for example, made almost $7 million in purchases through XPress Source in 2002 and 2003, saving $11 million during the two-year period. Movie Gallery has increased its purchases through XPress Source every year, saving even more money.

"Movie Gallery realizes profits from our revenues, plus we save them money on their purchases," Press says. "It's win-win for them."

Selling part ownership in a business isn't for every entrepreneur, and should not be done with just any buyer, Press says. "The whole key is getting a partner you can trust and [having] faith that they will do what they say they will do. We meet with them all the time, but for the day-to-day decisions they leave us alone. The reason we didn't want venture capital is that VCs want to run the company."

While Press and Mike were interested in having a hands-off buyer, they also were careful to sell a part of ECHO LLC to a company that brought more than money to the deal. Movie Gallery brought a large volume of business, which gave XPress Source stable, sustainable growth and credibility as Press and Mike went after other clients. Such a deal should be carefully structured through written contracts with each party fully aware of the limitations of the arrangement.

In order to make the procurement process less expensive and more efficient for clients, XPress Source depends heavily on software that can adjust to clients' processes instead of requiring clients to change for XPress Source. Each client may have thousands of vendors, which can be contacted almost instantly through XPress Source's software. Clients don't sacrifice information and flexibility in order to save money on purchasing supplies and other materials.

XPress Source doesn't just find the best and lowest-cost provider for each new contract for a client; it customizes an integrated strategy for finding sources of supplies for many different categories, if needed. If a client can benefit from electronic procurement, XPress Source sets it up. If contracts require monitoring and compliance checks, XPress Source does that too. In three years, XPress Source grew from 2 to 20 employees and revenues approaching $25 million. That type of growth would have been impossible if Press and Mike had been unwilling to part with a piece of the company to raise the needed capital for expansion.

94. STRATEGIC ALLIANCES

Companies can gain capital, innovation, new market
opportunities, and more by teaming up with other
companies that have specific competencies.

■ ■ ■

When aeronautical engineer George Brill started Talisen Technologies in St. Louis, Missouri, in 1991, he started providing engineering support to small companies. He met a group within Boeing Corporation that encouraged him to create a prototype for technology that would allow a company to communicate over a secure information technology (IT) network with its suppliers and customers. Boeing would be the first customer for this technology involving work with companies in foreign countries that purchased Boeing products.

"Boeing chose two small minority-owned businesses to be part of this industrial participation program," George says. "Boeing paid in U.S. dollars for what would normally be considered a franchise fee in other countries that helped us get started in the development. Boeing took the early-stage risk. That was very helpful to our growth."

For small companies like Talisen, a strategic alliance with a giant corporation can provide capital, credibility, distribution, and sales. But the large corporation isn't being altruistic. It also gains from the relationship by being able to bring new products to market more quickly for less cost than they could do internally. Communication is vital to making such alliances work. Each partner needs to understand what's driving the other participants so they can make sure everyone wins something in the deal. No matter how tempting it is to have ties with a major corporation, a small firm should reject an alliance that doesn't support its business goals. Ideally, a small company will cultivate several contacts within its giant partner. If a sole contact leaves the company, his or her successor might end the relationship, and the small business owner will have no inside champion to keep the alliance alive.

The Boeing alliance brought Talisen a million dollars in direct payments and several million dollars more in related business, George says. It has opened up markets in Europe, United Kingdom, and Australia. The company now has strategic alliances with Sun Microsystems and Hewlett-Packard and technical partnerships with Citrix and Plumtree Portal.

"We have diversified but still continue to grow with Boeing," George says. "It can be very tough dealing with a behemoth like Boeing. As we have passed through the $10 million sales threshold, it has put us on the radar screen of other companies that want to use our technology. We wouldn't have done that without Boeing."

When seeking alliances with major corporations, the entrepreneur needs to realize that a negative answer isn't always a final no, George says. "Look at the target company at multiple levels and keep taking multiple shots at the elephant. Such a huge customer has so many faces that it's hard to determine that you hit the right place. You must be persistent."

The entrepreneur needs to be creative when exploring strategic alliances. Some potential partners are obvious, but others may have voids in need of the smaller company's special expertise. In Talisen's case, the growing importance of IT security has opened up many possibilities.

The entrepreneur needs to keep in mind that the goal of alliances is to expand the business and increase capital by pooling management and financial resources with others. Each new alliance must have a role that adds something to the existing alliance portfolio or it should be rejected.

95. SMALL BUSINESS INVESTMENT COMPANIES

Small businesses in early-stage or growth situations can obtain debt or equity capital from special venture funds guaranteed by the U.S. Small Business Administration.

■ ■ ■

Ronald Thompson was an experienced manufacturing executive who in 1993 wanted to buy Midwest Stamping and Manufacturing Co. in Bowling Green, Ohio. The company made metal components for the bodies and frames of automobiles manufactured by Ford, Honda, Mercedes Benz, Nissan, Saturn, and others. Ron needed a total of more than $80 million including his own cash. A vital $2.5 million in equity was provided by TSG Ventures in Stamford, Connecticut, and Alliance Capital in Dallas, Texas, which were licensed Small Business Investment Companies (SBICs). TSG principals Duane Hill and Cleveland Christophe had known Ron for years and were confident in his judgment and abilities.

"I happened to know about SBICs going back to the '70s. This was the second venture I had financed using the SBIC industry as a source of equity or subordinated debt," Ron says. "I liked these particular funds I was working with. What you want in this situation is smart money, people who add value to the deal and who can understand the proposed transaction and make a decision quickly and efficiently whether they want to invest."

TSG not only brought strategic insights but other relationships to the transaction and both TSG and Alliance Capital had the capability to invest in later rounds of financing, if needed, Ron says.

In 1958 Congress created SBICs as privately owned and managed venture capital funds to provide equity and debt funding to small businesses that regular venture capitalists were ignoring. The government's interest was and is to increase jobs and tax revenues. The U.S. Small Business Administration issues SBIC licenses to experienced investment teams who raise from private sources either $5 million for a debenture fund or $10 million for an equity fund. For every $10 million raised, an SBIC can sell $20 million in debentures guaranteed by the SBA. The proceeds are invested or loaned to fast-growth companies that meet the federal definition of small businesses. The program has significantly impacted the U.S. venture market. Between 1960 and 2004, SBICs have put $36.5 billion into more than 109,000 deals. Among the companies that received SBIC infusions are Staples office supply superstores, Outback Steakhouse restaurant chain, and Apple computer.

"Before I acquired Midwest Stamping and Manufacturing Company, I was in the business of manufacturing railroad and defense material," Ron says. "The equity financing from TSG was important originally in structuring the acquisition transaction because it gave me credibility as I entered a new industry. We had our own equity, but having institutional equity investors added to our credibility. TSG also was helpful in negotiating terms of our senior and subordinated credit agreements. Since the acquisition, they've helped us evaluate strategic opportunities that have presented themselves. TSG has provided not only capital resources, but access to a very valuable network of human resources as well."

Ron has grown Midwest Stamping and Manufacturing from $64 million at the time of acquisition to more than $140 million.

As with any equity investment, Ron says, SBIC participation should be weighed for its strategic fit with others in the deal. "The entrepreneur really wants to make sure that his strategy is aligned with others who have a complete understanding what the growth needs are and what the ultimate exit will be."

96.

COMMUNITY DEVELOPMENT VENTURE CAPITAL

Some venture capital funds focus their investments in low-income areas in order to create jobs, build strong economies in distressed communities, and earn money for their investors.

■ ■ ■

When a group of angel investors led by Tom Reddoch wanted to buy Container Technologies Industries in Helenwood, Tennessee, in 2000, a venture capital fund would seem to be the last place they would look for capital. But SJF Ventures, formerly the Sustainable Jobs Fund, in Durham, North Carolina, is not a typical venture capital investor. It is one of about 80 community-development venture capital funds in the United States that have a duel purpose for their equity investments: profit for investors and social benefit. Some invest overseas; others in rural or low-income areas of the United States.

In SJF Ventures's case, it looks for companies in the eastern United States that can create jobs that don't require a college education, explains managing director Rick Larson. Therefore, many of its investments are in manufacturers and customer service businesses.

Container Technologies Industries was a good fit. Located in a rural Appalachian county with 31 percent poverty rate, it manufactures engineered steel containers for handling, storing, and transporting low-level radioactive waste. The buyers wanted to expand into new markets, promising SJF Ventures to increase the workforce from 30 to at least 45. Tom agreed to give SJF Ventures a 15 percent nongoverning stake in the company, renamed CTI LLC, for $266,500. The fund later invested another $30,000, increasing its ownership to 18 percent. While SJF Ventures typically wants a seat on a company's board of directors or the right to sit in and observe board meetings, the fund gave up its CTI board seat so that the company could meet requirements to take advantage of federal contracting preferences for small businesses in a U.S. Small Business Administration HUB-Zone (Historically Underutilized Business Zone). CTI's customers include the Oak Ridge National Laboratory.

"[SJF Ventures] had a very explicit due diligence process," Tom says. "They looked at our management team pretty closely. They also looked at the integrity of the other investors."

Rick says that a prospective investment must first meet SJF Ventures's job creation goals. "After that our due diligence is similar to other venture capitalists. We look for companies that can grow rapidly, have strong management, have something proprietary that will give the company an advantage over its competition, and that can attract a large enough market—$100 million to $500 million—so it can expand significantly."

SJF Ventures, started in 1999, initially would invest in start-up companies, but since 2001 will only consider businesses with revenues and customers that are poised for explosive growth. Its investors are large banks, which can get federal tax credits for such investments, the MacArthur Foundation, and others.

Community-development venture capital funds make smaller investments, typically $50,000 to $1.5 million, in companies than traditional venture funds, which average about $15 million. Their acceptable return is lower. For SJF Ventures, for example, it is three to five times the initial investment.

CTI has exceeded SJF Venture's expectations, becoming one of the best performers in the fund's $17 million portfolio. CTI has added 60 jobs and is the fastest growing employer in the area.

97. MEZZANINE VENTURE CAPITAL

Although later-stage venture financing is easier to win than
seed capital, investors have much higher performance
expectations for the receiving company.

■ ■ ■

Mobile phones are no longer just for voice transmissions, but devices for data, games, and text messaging. The complexity increases the risk of glitches and the need for software updates. Bitfone Corp. in Laguna Niguel, California, has more than 75 patents pending for technology that allows software and telecommunications companies to make updates and corrections over the air. On the strength of those patents, the company has raised more than $57 million from venture capital funds.

Nokia Venture Partners of Menlo Park, California, the venture arm of phone maker Nokia Corp., led the first round of funding of $6 million. Nokia participated with four other venture capital funds in the $19 million second round led by St. Paul Venture Capital of Minneapolis, Minnesota. After smaller rounds of $8 million and $1 million, Bitfone raised a $21 million third round of venture funding led by Prism Venture Partners of Westwood, Massachusetts, and involving many of the previous investors.

This pattern of venture funding is common for high-growth technology companies. Success is the best tactic for raising late-stage venture capital, sometimes called mezzanine or series B and series C funding. Companies that succeed in delivering on their initial business plan promises can raise substantially more money in later stages of development. Venture capitalists often prefer partnering with several other funds and corporate investors in various rounds of equity financing to share and mitigate the risk. Investors in the earlier round of financing are likely to participate in later rounds as well, although the venture fund bringing new money to the table usually leads the later round.

"But the later investors are looking for much more traction: revenues, corporate sponsors, and commercial deployment," says Bitfone chairman and chief executive Gene Wang. "In a series A round of funding, you can get by with a good idea and a good management team. By series C, they're looking for a good business plan, good revenue, and a good customer list."

Gene is one of the reasons for Bitfone's success at attracting venture capital. This is his third company as chief executive and his fourth start-up. In fact, the technology and management experience of his other management team members is measured not in years but in decades. The company's customers include Motorola, LG Electronics, and Sony Ericsson. Venture capitalists love to see such brand-name giants buying an investment company's products.

A company like Bitfone with such promising technology and early success in delivering on its promises doesn't have to be in the venture capital funds' backyard. Equity investing knows neither city nor country boundaries as the promise of huge returns become more and more real. However, Gene stresses that investors expect results.

Bitfone is carefully conserving cash by renting offices above a fitness gym rather than looking for highrise suites overlooking the Pacific Ocean. It is introducing new products worldwide and working on the next generation of over-the-air technology to keep potential competitors at bay. The equity capital also allows Bitfone to buy companies with compatible technology, which is faster than developing it. One such purchase was Mobile Diagnostix, whose software can detect mobile phone software problems.

98. LARGE CORPORATE INVESTORS

Private companies may invest in a small or young
company either as a money-making deal or to
access new technology or products.

■ ■ ■

Greig Altieri and his partners founded Vascular Control Systems in San Juan Capistrano, California, in 1998, to develop minimally invasive tools to treat a common female disorder characterized by excessive bleeding. From the beginning, they knew their most likely exit strategy would be acquisition by a large medical company. Medical technology can take years to develop, is riskier than many start-ups, and requires specialized knowledge to comprehend. Even a typical professional investor or venture capitalist is unlikely to understand well enough to feel comfortable with such investments. So once Vascular Control Systems's founders secured their intellectual property, they focused on venture capitalists who specialized in the medical device field and large corporations active in the medical and women's health industries. One of their early and continual contacts was with Johnson & Johnson Development Corp.

Several hundred companies worldwide, including Intel and DuPont, have corporate venture capital arms. They invest in emerging companies, which are better than these corporate giants at coming up with revolutionary technology and cutting-edge product improvements. They want to keep their ownership of a fledgling company below 20 percent so that they don't have to report in their financial statements an investment that might not pay off for years. These corporate investors are often more interested in strategic advantage than mere financial returns. They look for promising enterprises to bolster some existing product line or marketing direction. For Vascular Control Systems, Johnson & Johnson was a promising prospect because it was making a major play in the women's health market.

"Corporations are exceptional marketeers but not particularly adept at product development or improvement," Greig says.

Johnson & Johnson Development was an appealing target for another reason. One Vascular Control Systems founder had previously sold a company to a Johnson & Johnson division, which gave the start-up company an inside contact with the health giant, always a beneficial connection because relationships are so important in corporate investment decisions.

Still, Vascular Control Systems won three rounds of venture capital investments totaling more than $11 million for product development and preclinical trials before accepting $12.3 million from Johnson & Johnson Development for further clinical trials and approval from the U.S. Food and Drug Administration. Before accepting that investment, Greig talked with other major companies in the women's health arena and even had an offer that would have given that corporate investor first right of refusal to distribute Vascular Control Systems's products and to buy the company. Greig took that term sheet to Johnson & Johnson Development, which countered with a strictly equity investment offer, which is better for Vascular Control Systems's future.

"Price is part of the investment, but terms are more important," he says. "In recent years offers have had noxious terms that let the corporate investor get their money back and double dip by getting the product distribution rights."

If Greig does his job right and the clinical trials go as expected, Vascular Control Systems should have some offers for distribution rights and others for outright acquisition.

"Many companies are born out of a technology idea and go in search of a problem," Greig says. "We looked at the problem [of excessive uterine bleeding] and went in search of the best solution that would have market acceptance. We have a patent trail that will protect us from competitors for the next 10 to 12 years."

But long before that, Vascular Control Systems will likely be owned by a major corporation.

THE PUBLIC MARKETS

■ ■ ■

Eventually, some companies' capital needs outgrow their own profits, family resources, and professional investors' funds. Some want to use stock options as rewards and incentives for key employees and investors. The public markets offer a huge pool of capital, but it comes with burdensome regulations and constant pressure to grow revenues. Some managers of public companies fall into the trap of focusing on quarter-to-quarter results, rather than long-term growth. Reporting requirements for public companies are more expensive than many companies can bear.

99.   DIRECT STOCK OFFERING

Small companies can raise capital by selling stock to the
public without the full expense of registering with the
Securities and Exchange Commission.

■ ■ ■

Jim Bernau started a vineyard in Turner, Oregon, as a sole proprietor in 1983. Five years later he founded Willamette Valley Vineyards to produce premium to ultra premium varietal wines. A year later, Jim sold to the public the first shares in the company in order to fund the construction of the winery adjacent to the vineyards.

"It was really my business strategy from the beginning to marry the wine making with the desire to involve our customers in the business," Jim says. "We have almost 4,000 shareholders, mostly wine enthusiasts. They are evangelists for the company and our products."

A public offering registered with the Securities and Exchange Commission is an expensive undertaking involving accountants, attorneys, and underwriters. But the SEC, mindful of the prohibitive costs for small companies, provides several exemptions from the regular initial public offering. An intrastate offering allows a company to sell its shares in its home state only to residents of that state. A private offering sells shares only to sophisticated investors who have enough financial knowledge and expertise to evaluate the merits and risks of such an offering. Jim used Regulation A, which allows the sale of up to $5 million in stock within a 12-month period. He didn't have to register his offering, but he did have to create an offering circular—similar to a prospectus—that provided basic business and financial information to help investors evaluate the merits of the deal.

The marketing of shares in a direct stock offering is substantially different from standard IPOs. You're selling, usually face-to-face, with individuals who are friends, family, customers, and suppliers. It requires marketing techniques similar to direct selling of products and services. IPOs, on the other hand, are sold through underwriters who make their connections to institutional investors and to brokerage firms whose stock brokers, in turn, sell to individual investors.

"Willamette Valley Vineyards's affinity group strategy has to be real. You have to have a tremendous amount of trust," Jim says.

His shareholders don't merely buy securities; they buy a role in the company. Many of them are retired and consider their investment to be good recreation as well as a good investment. Nine out of ten of them live within 50 miles of the company headquarters. They help gather the grapes and persuade restaurants to buy the wine and even deliver the bottles to the customers. They become registered wine servers so that they can pour wine at festivals in Oregon, one of Willamette Valley Vineyards's distribution channels.

However, Jim isn't sure he—or any other small companies—can afford to use Regulation A stock offerings in the future, primarily because of the 2002 passage of the Sarbanes-Oxley Act adopted by Congress to reform corporate governance and financial disclosures after the Enron scandal. The law does not exempt small companies, and the reporting and auditing costs a bundle.

"For several years the regulatory costs of accountants and attorneys have escalated, and with Sarbanes-Oxley the professional fees for auditors is overwhelming," Jim says. "We have revenues of $7.5 million and this could wipe out our profitability. The new law is a great disincentive for small companies to raise capital in this way."

Organizations representing small businesses are lobbying for some regulatory relief for companies with annual revenues of less than $50 million.

100. PUBLIC STOCK OFFERING

Selling company equity to the public can raise more money
than other sources, but the owners surrender more
control than other means of acquiring capital.

■ ■ ■

Henry Samueli and Henry Nicholas, both PhDs in engineering, foresaw the explosion in high-speed communications, and launched Broadcom Corp. in Irvine, California, in 1991. The company made superfast chips for cable modems and digital television set-top boxes. The two Henrys, as employees called them, financed the company themselves rather than seeking venture capital or other equity investments. They won contracts for their technology-pushing products over the next seven years while positioning Broadcom for an initial public stock offering in 1998.

Relatively few of the more than 24 million U.S. businesses are realistic candidates for an IPO, which is a complex process that must start long before the stock goes up for public sale. Generally a company must have a strong management team, a growth rate higher than its industry's average, innovative products or services with a large and immediate market, and stable and predictable operations including adequate internal financial reporting and accounting controls. Huge sales and profits aren't a requirement if a company has strong potential. Broadcom had annual sales of $37 million and had actually lost money in 1997, but the U.S. stock market during that period was exploding with the excitement over technology, especially Internet-related offerings.

An IPO has been a favorite exit strategy for venture capitalists, depending on the strength of the stock market. The number of IPOs in the years 2000 to 2003 was terrible following the collapse of the Internet bubble. Prior to an IPO, a company must qualify with the Securities and Exchange Commission and convince an investment banker—often several pool their resources—to underwrite the offering. The underwriter markets the stock and sets the initial selling price at what it thinks the market will pay. In Broadcom's case, even the underwriter was surprised by the public's appetite. The initial selling price per share was $24, double the price initially anticipated. Broadcom sold 2.75 million, grossing $66 million, and existing shareholders sold 750,000 shares, grossing $18 million. The two Henrys retained majority ownership of Broadcom and made $6.5 million each on their sale of shares. It was one of the hottest IPOs of 1998. An IPO is also an expensive way to raise capital. The underwriters and lawyers take a sizeable percentage of the money raised.

The public offering was intended to raise money for expansion and provide a way for key Broadcom employees to sell their company stock easily, called shareholder liquidity, Henry Samueli says. "They had worked so hard for seven years and needed to be rewarded for that."

Broadcom could have continued growing slowly by funding operations on internal profits, but the public offering catapulted the company into rapid acquisition of more than 20 companies with compatible technologies over the next few years and annual revenues exceeding $1.6 billion.

That financial flexibility and growth comes at a steep price, Henry Samueli says. "There [is] lots of downside to being public. You are always under a microscope."

Public companies have hundreds or thousands of "bosses"—the shareholders who apply pressure for increased growth. Much information must be disclosed in public filings, which can tip competitors to company products and strategies. Also, founders rarely retain control over the company's operations and vision. Henry Samueli, who remains chairman and chief technology officer of Broadcom, is an exception. Still he is not the sole decision maker determining Broadcom's future. "You can't run a company quarter to quarter; you won't survive, but you completely lose all privacy," he says.

101. DUTCH AUCTION OF STOCK

Instead of an investment banker setting an asking price
for stock, an auction establishes the "true" market
price based on what buyers are willing to pay.

■ ■ ■

Since Sergey Brin and Larry Page started the Internet search engine
Google Inc. in Mountain View, California, in 1998, they have sought to run
their company differently than most corporations. They stressed such be-
liefs as the value of democracy on the Web and making money without doing evil. So it was no surprise when they decided to sell stock in Google in
2004 that they chose an unconventional way to do it. The founders wanted
to avoid some of the IPO abuses of the late 1990s in which a company's
stock would double or triple in price the first day, which made favored institutional investors rich at the expense of later buyers. They chose what is
called a Dutch auction.

Traditionally, underwriters would be embarrassed if the newly public
company's shares rose dramatically because it would indicate they hadn't
gotten all the money they could for the client company. However, in the
late 1990s, the technology boom encouraged an opening day "pop" in
price, which richly rewarded those who bought at the opening price and
flipped their stocks to subsequent buyers. The company going public
didn't raise all it could, but few complained until the tech bubble burst in
early 2000.

Sergey and Larry made it clear that neither they—as the major shareholders in the world's most popular Internet search service—nor Google
Inc. needed the capital that would be raised by an initial public offering. In
fact, they created two classes of voting stock to make sure they and chief
executive Eric Schmidt would control decision making after the company
went public. The pair also wanted individual investors to have an equal
chance at the opening price with major investment houses and institutional
investors. An initial investor would be allowed to buy as few as five shares.
The primary motivation for going public, the pair said, was to provide their
employees and venture capital backers a means to make a profit from their

sweat and capital equity in the company's early years. In fact, Larry told potential shareholders that if they were "hoping to capture profits shortly after our Class A common stock begins trading, [they] may be disappointed. We would request our shareholders take the long-term view. A management team distracted by a series of short-term targets is as pointless as a dieter stepping on a scale every half hour."

Because Google was the most hotly anticipated IPO in years, its Dutch auction didn't work exactly the way this method typically does. In a typical auction, a company states the number of shares it will sell on a specific date. Google didn't reveal the number of shares or the date of its IPO until August 18, 2004, the day before the event. In July, the company reported to the Securities and Exchange Commission that the sale price would likely be $108 to $135. And then on August 18, Google said the price would be $85 to $95. Would-be investors had to register first and then name their price when Google opened bidding on August 13.

The day of Google's IPO, the first shares sold at $85, raising a net $1.7 billion for the company, and the price rose to $108.34 by the close of first-day trading, an 18 percent increase. That boost indicates that Google didn't entirely maximize its public offering. However, investors take a risk to buy a company's stock before its value is determined on the open market because they believe they will make a profit by selling to future buyers. A successful auction leaves some value as a reward for the first public investors.

WHAT COMMERCIAL LENDERS WANT

It is tempting to think of bankers as money ogres, ruthlessly and carelessly tossing aside your perfectly good plea for capital to start or grow your business. But in fairness, commercial lenders have a fiduciary responsibility—meaning they can go to jail if they abuse it—to their depositors and shareholders to invest their money wisely. They are more risk averse than equity investors and entrepreneurs.

Commercial lenders, like most other people in business, tend to do business with people they know and trust. It pays to develop a banking relationship before you need a loan. Find a banker who understands your industry and type of business. Make an appointment and share a copy of your business plan. Keep in touch. Bankers hate surprises. Also recognize that you can be a great customer for a bank. Have the self-confidence to shop around for one that can be a good partner in your growth.

When you approach commercial lenders for a loan, you will have greater success if you can prove to them that you have most or all of the following:

- *Ability to repay the loan.* Put in your business plan how the business will use the loan proceeds to add to capacity or grow revenues in order to repay the loan. Or, illustrate how current cash flow is sufficient to cover loan payments.
- *Collateral.* Lenders want real estate or other valuable items that they can sell to recoup their money if the borrower defaults on the loan. Often equipment or computers are not good collateral because their value depreciates too rapidly or there is no resale market for them.
- *Owners' or managers' experience.* Lenders look at the track record of management for evidence that they know what they are doing so

the company will succeed in the future. If the lender lacks any history with the borrowing company, it helps the financier to know the managers have run other businesses successfully in the past.

- *Credit history.* If the entrepreneurs have faithfully repaid loans in the past, they are more likely to get the new loan.
- *Borrower's contribution.* Lenders like the borrower to have cash in the project too. A borrower with nothing personal to lose can more easily walk away from debt.
- *Character.* Lenders will more readily work with business owners who have a track record of integrity and honesty. Without character, you might have the money and still not repay the debt.

WHAT PROFESSIONAL EQUITY INVESTORS WANT

Equity investors are people who buy a piece of the business ranging from the owner's mom to venture capitalists to shareholders. These groups want vastly different things. The professional investors—the angels and venture capitalists—are important links in the capital chain helping to develop new products and services and to grow the American economy. One study reported that venture-backed companies have created ten million jobs and $1.7 trillion in revenue from 1970 to 2003.

First, relatively few companies appeal to these professional investors. Ideally, professional investors want young, fast-growing companies that can dominate a market, pay a high return on investment, and allow investors to exit within three to seven years. Only a few thousand firms receive venture investments each year.

The angels tend to invest smaller amounts of money at earlier stages of a company's development. Venture capitalists usually are the next step of development with larger amounts of money.

Both types of investors want some hands-on participation in their investments. They look for companies to which they can bring special expertise and relationships that help the ventures develop. Many entrepreneurs resent this participation as interference, but the angels and venture capitalists often have successful experiences in other companies.

The characteristics that venture investors want in a potential investment include:

- *Strong management team.* Angels and venture capitalists look first at the quality and experience of a company's management. They may insist on putting stronger members in some positions.

- *Intellectual property.* This comprises ideas or developments that can be protected from competitors and raise barriers to new entrants in a market.
- *Market dominance.* Venture investors would rather a company be capable of capturing 80 percent of a $100 million niche market than 1 percent of a $100 billion market.
- *Strong potential for rapid and high growth.* During the dot-com era of the late 1990s, venture capitalists wanted 200 percent growth and a strategy that allowed them to take their investment out in 18 months. Expectations have eased considerably, but they still like to see 40 to 50 percent annual growth.
- *Industries with which they are comfortable.* Professional investors have various fields with which they are most comfortable. Some specialize in biotechnology, others in health care, for example. Few are interested in restaurants because of the high failure rate. Some industries' popularity ebbs and flows, such as telecommunications and Web retailing, which were hot in the late '90s and cool several years later.
- *Relationships.* Virtually no professional investors will take a chance on a company or entrepreneur who has not been introduced by a trusted colleague or advisor.

FORMAT FOR THE BUSINESS PLAN

Because the written business plan is so important in obtaining capital, understand the information that lenders and investors expect to find in this document. Here is the general format to follow.

TITLE PAGE

Also called the cover sheet, this page should contain the name of the company, street address, telephone number, and Web site address; the names, titles, and contact information for all owners and officers; the date the plan was prepared; and the name of the person who prepared it. Many companies number each copy of the business plan and track who sees the document because it contains proprietary information.

EXECUTIVE SUMMARY

This relatively brief portion pulls together the information in the plan and is the last part written, although it is placed first in the document. It gives a synopsis of what the business does, where it is heading, how it will get there, and why it will succeed.

TABLE OF CONTENTS

The page listing makes it easier to find specific information within the plan.

THE BUSINESS

This section describes the enterprise and its goals. It explains the legal structure, division of responsibilities for key executives, competitive advantages, protections for any intellectual property, methods of distribution, and details such as hours of operation.

MARKETING

The marketing section describes the company's products or services, identifies customer demand, details the size and location of the target market, and describes how the company will attract and increase market share. This section also explains the pricing strategy and methods for advertising.

FINANCIAL ANALYSIS

This section provides a budget and balance sheet of assets and liabilities and identifies the breakeven point and expected return on investment. If the plan is being used to get a loan, this section explains how the proceeds will be used and the debt repaid. If the plan is for potential equity investors, this section explains how the proceeds will be used and the investors' anticipated return on investment.

OPERATIONS

This section describes how the company operates day to day. It explains personnel procedures, production, and delivery of products or services. It lists all insurance, lease, or rental agreements and essential equipment. Actual copies of these documents are in the next section.

SUPPORTING DOCUMENTS

In order to keep the previous sections brief and readable, supporting information for business plan assertions are placed in this section. If lenders or investors want to know such details, they have the information but it doesn't bog down the main part of the plan.

RESOURCES

The following companies, agencies, and Web sites provide information, technical assistance, counseling, and/or capital for U.S. private businesses:

ACCION USA, 56 Roland Street, Suite 300, Boston, MA 02129, 617-625-7080; e-mail: info@accionusa.org; Web site http://www.accionusa.org. Provides microloans to business owners who can't qualify for traditional financing.

Angel Capital Association, http://www.angelcapitalassociation.org. Details information about angel groups.

Community Development Venture Capital Alliance, 330 Seventh Avenue, 19th Floor, New York, NY 10001, 212-594-6747; http://www.cdvca.org. Trade association for venture capital funds that invest in low-income and economically distressed communities.

Ewing Marion Kauffman Foundation, 4801 Rockhill Road, Kansas City, MO 64110, 816-932-1000, http://www.kauffman.org and http://www.entre world.org. Provides support and data about angel investing, entrepreneurial education, and more.

International Franchise Association, 1350 New York Avenue NW, #900, Washington, DC 20005, 202-628-8000, http://www.franchise.org. An organization of franchisors, franchisees, and service providers.

National Association of Government Guaranteed Lenders, 424 South Squires Street, #130, Stillwater, OK 74074, 405-377-4022, http://www .naggl.org.

National Association of Small Business Investment Companies, 666 11th Street NW, Washington, DC 20001, 202-628-5055, http://www.nasbic .com. Provides information about the small business investment company program and member companies.

National Business Incubator Association, 703-593-4331, http://www.nbia .org. Provides information about business incubators and services throughout the United States.

National Rural Development Partnership, USDA/RBS, Room 5045-S 1400 Independence Avenue SW, Washington, DC 20250-3201, 202-690-4730, http://www.rurdev.usda.gov. Offers loan programs for businesses in rural areas under the U.S. Department of Agriculture.

National Venture Capital Association, 1655 North Fort Myer Drive, Suite 850, Arlington, VA 22209, 703-524-2549, fax 703-524-3940, http://www .nvca.org. Trade association for the venture capital industry that tracks investing activity and lists members on its Web site.

Out of Your Mind . . . And Into the Marketplace, http://www.business-plan .com. Publisher of business planning books and software.

Pratt's Guide to Private Equity Sources and *Pratt's Guide to Venture Capital Sources.* Books updated regularly with money sources and service providers for entrepreneurial ventures, published by Securities Data Publishing, a division of Thomson Financial, http://www.thomson.com.

SCORE, 800-634-0245, http://www.score.org. More than 10,000 volunteers in 389 chapters nationwide that provide free one-on-one counseling and low-cost workshops for business owners and people who want to start businesses.

SJF Ventures, 400 West Main Street, #604, Durham, NC 27701, 919-530-1177, http://www.sjfund.com. Invests in fast-growth ventures in the eastern United States.

U.S. Small Business Administration, 800-UASK-SBA (800-827-5722), http://www.sba.gov. Government agency that advises the President and Congress about federal issues that impact small businesses.

SBA microloan program lenders. For a list of nonprofit community intermediaries, go to the SBA's Web site, http://www.sba.gov, click on "financing your business," then click on "small business lenders," then click on "SBA microlenders by state," and then click on your state.

Tech Coast Angels, http://www.techcoastangels.com. One of the largest angel investor groups with three chapters in Los Angeles, San Diego, and Orange counties in California.

U-Start Incubator, 4 Nott Terrace, Schenectady, NY 12308, 518-631-0475, http://www.incubator.union.edu. Technology-focused incubator at Union College.

WEB SITES OF BUSINESSES IN THIS BOOK

1. Best Made Mattress Co. Inc., http://www.bestmademattress.com and http://www.simplepedic.com
2. Lumetique Inc., http://www.lumetique.com, and The Venture Alliance, http://www.tvausa.com
3. CharterAuction.com Inc., http://www.charterauction.com
4. Cunningham & Co., http://www.cunninghamcomp.com
5. Pinnacle Services Inc., http://www.pinnacleservices.org
7. Mama Dip's Kitchen, http://www.mamadips.com
8. Norfolk Beverage Co., http://www.norfolkbeverage.com
9. Back to Basics Learning Dynamics Inc., http://www.backtobasics learning.com
10. Iron Frog Productions, http://www.ironfrog.com
12. PR/PR, http://www.prpr.net
13. Material Possessions, http://www.quiltessentials.com
14. Natural Farms Inc., http://www.naturalfarms.org
15. Orange County Interior Fashions, http://www.ocinfashions.com
16. GR Capital, http://www.grcapital.com
17. Meadowood Bed and Breakfast, http://www.blueridgebedandbreak fast.net
18. Southwest Financial Services, http://www.sffinancialgroup.com
19. Warwick Construction Inc., http://www.warwickconstruction.com
20. Media Stage, http://www.mediastage.com
21. Frontier Steel Co., http://www.frontiersteel.com
22. The Art House, http://www.artforkids.biz
23. CTI/Valueline, http://www.ctivalueline.com
24. Jarrett Logistics Systems, http://www.jarrettlogistics.com

25. E-Z Bag Snap Ring LLC, http://www.bagwizard.com
27. The QuickSource, http://www.thequicksource.com
28. Colarelli Construction, http://www.colarelliconstruction.com
29. Skyline Forest Resources Inc., http://www.tetonwest.com
30. Craftsmen Industries, http://www.craftsmenind.com
31. Chem-Dry, http://www.chemdryusa.com
32. Quantum Sphere, http://www.qsinano.com
33. The Growing Room Child Development Centers, http://www.grow
    ingroomga.com
35. iMortgage Services, http://www.imortgageservices.com
36. The Property Bureau, http://www.propertybureau.com
37. Company Nurse, http://www.companynurse.com
38. Aktino Inc., http://www.aktino.com
39. Freeze LLC, http://www.freezellc.com and http://www.freeze.com
40. Kott Koatings Inc., http://www.kottkoatings.com
41. Snapware Corp., http://www.snapwareusa.com
42. ATC International Inc., http://www.atcinternational.net
43. Olympic Hot Tub Co., http://www.olympichottub.com
44. Archibald's Inc., http://www.archibalds.biz
45. ReCONNstruction Center, http://www.reconnstructioncenter.org
46. Principor Communications, http://www.principor.com
47. Vision Technologies Inc., http://www.visiontech.biz
48. Davin Wheel Co., http://www.davinwheels.com
49. 3D Research Corp., http://www.3drc.com
50. Mickman Brothers, http://www.mickman.com
51. Media Storm, http://www.mediastorm.biz
52. British American Auto Care Inc., http://www.britishamericanauto
    .com
53. Rising Medical Solutions Inc., http://www.risingms.com
54. Arose Recruiting Co. Inc., http://www.aroserecruiting.com
55. International Delivery Solutions LLC, http://www.idstrac.com
56. Stolhand Heating & Air Conditioning Inc., http://www.stolhandheat
    andair.com
57. Cougar Turbine Supply LP, http://www.cougarturbine.com

58. Rowland Companies, http://www.rowlandcompanies.com

59. Treetop Solutions, http://www.treetopsolutions.com

61. Buck Knives, http://www.buckknives.com

62. Dakota Pharmacy, http://www.dakotarx.com

63. Airporter Shuttle/Bellair Charters, http://www.airporter.com

64. Premier Pet Products, http://www.premier.com

66. Horizon Business Systems, http://www.horizon-business.net

67. Black River Produce, http://www.blackriverproduce.com

68. Mott's Miniatures & Dollhouse Shop, http://www.minishop.com

69. C.W. Keller & Associates Inc., http://www.cwkeller.com

70. Fabtech, http://www.fabtechmotorsports.com

71. Mansion House, http://www.mvmansionhouse.com

72. Thralow Inc., http://www.binoculars.com, http://www.telescopes
    .com, and http://www.peepers.com

73. All Season Photography, http://www.allseasonphoto.com

74. Advance Med LLC, http://www.advancemed.org

75. South Texas Vocational Technical Institute, http://www.stvt.edu

76. Action Mold, http://www.actionmold.com

78. Summit Aeronautics Group, http://www.summitaero.com

79. IJ Research Inc., http://www.ijresearch.com

80. Machine Solutions Inc., http://www.machinesolutions.org

81. Eliot James Enterprises, http://www.ejeinc.com

82. The Alliance Portfolio, http://www.theallianceportfolio.com

83. JMP Creative, http://www.jmpcreative.com

84. Factfinders, http://www.yourinfogenie.com

85. Meyerhof's Fine Catering, http://www.meyerhofs.com

87. Something Moore, http://www.somethingmoore.com

88. Academy of Tutoring Professionals, http://www.etutorme.com

89. National Gaming Association, http://www.ngasports.com

90. Plums Café & Catering, http://www.plumscafe.com

91. Systems Paving Inc., http://www.systemspaving.com

92. iPayables Inc., http://www.ipayables.com

93. Xpress Source/ECHO LLC Co., http://www.xpresssource.com

94. Talisen Technologies, http://www.talisentech.com

96. Container Technologies Industries LLC, http://www.containertech
    nologies.com

97. Bitfone Corp., http://www.bitfone.com

99. Willamette Valley Vineyards, http://www.willamettevalleyvineyards
    .com

100. Broadcom Corp., http://www.broadcom.com

101. Google, http://www.google.com

INDEX